PENGUIN BOOKS

The Public Confessions of a Middle-aged Woman

'I want to be this funny. I want to be as funny, witty, sceptical and as unrepentantly cynical as Susan Lilian Townsend' *Journal*

'Proof once more that Townsend is one of the funniest writers around' *The Times*

'Anyone who loved *The Secret Diary of Adrian Mole* will enjoy this collection of witty and sharply observed jottings from the inimitable Sue Townsend. Great stuff' *OK!*

'Sue Townsend is eloquent, wise and above all full of fun . . . whether she's happy, nostalgic or just plain angry, her wit and honesty make her an unmissable read' *Sainsbury's Magazine*

'It's as if Townsend has caught our idiosyncrasies on candid camera and is showing a rerun of all the silly clips' *Time Out*

'What a fantastic advertisement for middle-age – it can't be bad if it's this funny' *Heat*

'Townsend has such a witty way with words that it makes her consistently amusing . . . a welcome addition to any bookshelf' *Hello!*

'Townsend is every woman's favourite Everywoman' *Good Housekeeping*

Sue Townsend, with *The Secret Diary of Adrian Mole Aged 13¾* (1982) and *The Growing Pains of Adrian Mole* (1984), was Britain's bestselling author of the 1980s. Her hugely successful novels are *Rebuilding Coventry* (1988), *True Confessions of Adrian Albert Mole, Margaret Hilda Roberts and Susan Lilian Townsend* (1989), *Adrian Mole: From Minor to Major* (1991), *The Queen and I* (1992), *Adrian Mole: The Wilderness Years* (1993), *Ghost Children* (1997), *Adrian Mole: The Cappuccino Years* (1999), *The Public Confessions of a Middle-aged Woman* (2001) and *Number Ten* (2002). Most of her books are published by Penguin. She is also well known as a playwright. She lives in Leicester.

The Public Confessions of a Middle-aged Woman

SUE TOWNSEND

PENGUIN BOOKS

PENGUIN BOOKS

Published by the Penguin Group
Penguin Books Ltd, 80 Strand, London WC2R ORL, England
Penguin Putnam Inc., 375 Hudson Street, New York, New York 10014, USA
Penguin Books Australia Ltd, 250 Camberwell Road,
Camberwell, Victoria 3124, Australia
Penguin Books Canada Ltd, 10 Alcorn Avenue, Toronto, Ontario, Canada M4V 3B2
Penguin Books India (P) Ltd, 11 Community Centre,
Panchsheel Park, New Delhi – 110 017, India
Penguin Books (NZ) Ltd, Cnr Rosedale and Airborne Roads,
Albany, Auckland, New Zealand
Penguin Books (South Africa) (Pty) Ltd, 24 Sturdee Avenue,
Rosebank 2196, South Africa

Penguin Books Ltd, Registered Offices: 80 Strand, London WC2R ORL, England

www.penguin.com

First published by Michael Joseph 2001
Published in Penguin Books 2003
1

Copyright © Sue Townsend, 2001
All rights reserved

These pieces first appeared in Sainsbury's *The Magazine* between 1993 and 2001

The moral right of the author has been asserted

Set in Monotype Dante
Printed in England by Clays Ltd, St Ives plc

Contents

Introduction

This collection of monthly pieces represents a sort of sanitized autobiography and is carefully entitled the *Public Confessions*. (the *Private Confessions* will never be written.) Before I wrote the first column, I made a few rules for myself.

- I would not exploit members of my family.
- I would not write about dogs or cats.
- I would not quote taxi drivers.
- I would steer clear of using the personal pronouns: I, Me, Myself.

I have broken most of these rules in every column I write. My husband features heavily in these pages as a long-suffering but patient man. Bill and Max (dog and cat respectively) appear in later columns more often than I would like, and a quote from a taxi driver called Elias got both me and him in trouble with that Great Man, the ludicrous Jeffrey Archer.

Elias and I got to know each other well as we crossed and re-crossed the Greek island of Skyros, from airport to harbour, in a search for my lost husband. During one journey Elias told me that once he was hired by Jeffrey

Archer to drive him, Mary and their guests on a trawl of the Skyrian pottery shops. Apparently, the Great Man has an impressive collection, though it has to be said that not everybody shares his taste. Elias would meet the great man's yacht at the harbour, and off they would go. Naturally I was intrigued and asked what the great Archer was like on his holidays. Elias said, 'Sue, he talk to me like *"dog"*.'

I was indignant that Archer could show such disrespect to Elias (who had a genuine university degree, and good manners, unlike Archer).

I felt a prick of unease when I wrote this. When I next returned to Skyros I was astonished to be told by Elias that Archer had rung him from England to complain.

'I don't care, Sue,' said Elias, laughing, 'He is pig.'

I agreed to work for Sainsbury's *The Magazine* after a delightful dinner at the RAC club with Delia Smith and the editor, Michael Wynn-Jones. I had never met either of them before. All I knew was that they were starting a new magazine and wanted to talk to me about it. My heart sank at the phrase 'new magazine'.

This innocent-sounding phrase is usually a code. It means give me your hard-earned money, I will 'invest' it in setting up a publication that nobody wants to read, and after much heartbreak and hard work I will set fire to your money, and cast the burning notes into the wind. Ensuring that you will never see your money again.

There was a great deal of laughter and almost as much liquor. After saying over the soup that I couldn't possibly fit in any more work, I talked myself into it during the main course. I heard myself gush over coffee that I would be delighted to provide them with 800 words a month. 800 words was *nothing*. I could write them on the train from

Leicester to St Pancras, or in the kitchen while I waited for my rock cakes to harden in the oven. I saw myself seated at a pavement café with an elegant notepad and inky pen, honing and polishing 800 wise and witty words.

Forgive me if I larf. These 800 words have mostly been dragged out of me kicking and screaming. (Which reminds me, one of the rules was that I would also avoid clichés, like the plague.)

I don't think I have ever delivered the 800 on time. This is the most disgraceful confession of all. In fact, I have no right to call myself a professional writer. The pros get up early and go to their study. After a moment's thought they type out 800 lucid double-spaced words. After a little light editing this document is sent to the editor with a chirpy comment on a compliments slip. I'm convinced other columnists do not do as I do – lie in bed quaking with fear, gnashing my teeth, telling anyone who will listen (few lately), 'I can't do it. I've got nothing to write about.' In my own defence, and on the advice of my live-in therapist, Dr Eagleburger, I should explain that I work under certain restrictions. Magazines with high production values such as *Sainsbury's Magazine* cannot be thrown together overnight. We are a very long way from the Tortoise Society's newsletter type of thing. My words have to be written three months ahead, so topicality is out and I can't take advantage of national events.

I do hope that you enjoy these pieces. Personally, me, myself, I haven't been able to re-read them again.

Sue Townsend
Leicester
July 2001

Aga Saga

Two years ago I saw my first Aga. It was in the home of a mad journalist and was covered in twenty years of accumulated grease but it was love at first sight. The warmth, the strength, the classic lines, the fact that Agas are always hot and ready for action appealed to me. The Aga has many of the qualities one would like, but so rarely gets, from a lover.

I sent for a brochure and slobbered over it for days. I became conversant with Aga terminology, 'the two-oven', 'the four-oven', 'the simmering plate'. Eventually the decision was made. I rang up the supplier and tried to order a 'two-oven in cream please'. A voice on the other end of the phone informed me that an interview would be necessary first to see if I was 'suitable'. You'd have thought I'd been trying to adopt a baby or get a boy into Eton.

As the day of my interview drew near, I began to worry. Would the supplier consider me and my husband suitable owners? We drank and smoked and kept late hours. Would we be *turned down*?

We needn't have worried, the supplier was not interested

in our morals or our views on apartheid. He merely busied himself with a tape measure, asked a few pertinent questions about the chimney flue, took a deposit and left.

Cunningly I was away from home during the run-up to the installation, the flue had to be lined, fitted units ripped out, the kitchen floor strengthened, and a gas pipe re-routed. When I returned my husband and I stood arm in arm and looked at the gap where the Aga would be. Like first-time expectant parents we talked about how our lives would change.

I was also away on the day it was installed but I phoned throughout the day, anxious for news of its progress. At 6 p.m. my daughter answered and in gloomy tones she said, 'It's in, it's horrible, and I'm scared of it.' You'd have thought she was describing an evil monster. My husband came on the phone. 'I love it,' he enthused. 'I can't take my hands off it, it's beautiful.' I felt a twinge of jealousy and hurried home to meet my rival, Ms Aga. And there she was, all gleaming chrome and cream bodywork: the Marilyn Monroe of the cooker world. My husband was already her slave, producing cheese scones and chocolate sponge cakes from her sultry depths. He was a man besotted.

A few days later we received an invitation to a 'New Aga Owners evening'. There was to be a cookery demonstration and the 'opportunity' to buy some Aga cookware. My husband was on the phone at once confirming our places.

The evening arrived, we dressed carefully, anxious not to look like Aga louts. We took our seats in the back row. In front of us in a mock-up kitchen was a 'four-oven' Aga. The seats began to fill up around us. It was an exceptionally well dressed audience, we would not have been out of place in the Royal Opera House. The tension grew, then at

8 p.m. prompt the lights went down and the demonstrator welcomed us to the show.

Within seconds my husband and I were giggling uncontrollably – the woman had the most extraordinary voice. She would start a sentence sounding like the Queen, and finish with an impression of Pauline Fowler from *EastEnders*. We managed to pull ourselves together after five minutes but by then it was clear that the demonstrator was using this cookery demonstration as a sort of free therapy session.

As she handed out sausage rolls fresh from the oven, she related sad tales of her teenagers' outrages and confided that her husband refused to use the Aga, couldn't boil an egg, and spent most of his time in the pub. However, her smile never slipped and the food she turned out was delicious.

My husband's romance with Ms Aga is still on, although she is not as young as she was. She's stained and scratched but she's always there, ready for him. And when he shouts, 'Darling I'm home,' as he comes through the door, I'm not sure whom he's greeting.

War on Slugs

A bad week; first I had a letter from a bankrupt Bulgarian, an ex-private eye, who threatened to shoot himself unless I sent him $28,000 (I'm not making this up!), and now the slugs have launched their summer campaign. If you denote a slight paranoia in my reference to slugs, I can just say in my defence that last year I came down to find slug trails, not only in my garden but in my living room!

They had promenaded past one sofa, circled the coffee table, and then headed towards the television and video. I felt like the Last of the Mohicans as I followed their glistening tracks but, unlike our American Indian brothers and sisters (who love all living things), I had only hatred in my heart for the squelching molluscs. I poked a toasting fork under the television table (bought in a moment of madness – a tastefully written card on it had said, 'Antique TV and Video Stand'). After poking about fruitlessly, I gave up and concluded the slugs had had a good look around and gone back into the garden to feast on my tender young plants – possibly to punish me for my bad taste in furniture.

I used to be known for my gormlessness, my refusal to

think badly of anyone, my passivity, but slugs have changed my character.

After the living-room incident, I toughened up. I turned into a serial killer. I read up on slugs and gathered the tools of destruction: cans of lager, empty Diet Coke bottles, slug pellets, a torch, a new pair of washing-up gloves and a child's bucket and spade.

First, I laid my lager trap: half of an inverted Diet Coke bottle (top downwards and tightly screwed) was sunk into the earth. A quarter of a pint of lager was poured inside, then the rim of the bottle was cunningly disguised with good, soft soil. I then drank the rest of the lager.

When darkness fell I went inside, to write and to wait. It was hard to concentrate. I was nervous. After all, it was the first time I'd planned a mass murder.

It was around midnight when I tiptoed into the garden, wearing the rubber gloves and carrying the torch. Me and the slugs keep late hours. We walk on the wild side. I heard them first, a horrible sound of unbridled greed. They were gorging on my plants, tearing at them with their thousands of teeth. I switched the torch on and caught them in the beam. If they'd been humans, they'd have raised their hands in the air and said, 'It's a fair cop, guv,' but being slugs they ignored me and carried on destroying the tender nicotiana plants I'd grown from seed. Enraged, I hurried to fetch my little spade meant for making sand castles, but now about to be used for a less innocent pastime – that of ferrying slugs to their death. On my way, I passed the lager pit. Slugs were gathered around the rim like boozers at a bar, others had fallen in and were drunk or dead. I'm not sure, but I may have cackled.

My next patrol was at 3 a.m. when more victims were

claimed. It was a night of revenge and retribution. Dawn was breaking when I eventually crawled into bed, tired but triumphant. But sleep evaded me. I was tormented by the thought that although I had culled dozens, there must be hundreds, if not thousands of them still out there. It was then that the slug obsession began to take hold of me.

The next day, my children came round and found me counting the dead. They were horrified. There were cries of, 'How cruel!' and 'Poor things!' and 'How could you?' None of my children had gardens at the time, so it was useless trying to explain to them that flowers and shrubs were superior forms of life. I kept my silence and eventually they drifted back indoors (like most young people, they distrust fresh air). When I joined them, I noticed them looking at me with a new respect. Their daffy, soft-touch mother was gone for ever. In her place was a slug killer. A woman fully capable of refusing hand-outs, a grandmother no longer available for last-minute baby-sitting duties.

Like all obsessives, I've become a bore. I've just said to my husband, 'Did you know slugs breed by firing aphro-disiac darts into each other?' I think he muttered, 'Of course' but it may have been 'Divorce'.

The Slob's Holiday

My husband and I went to Reno for our holiday last year. The children were alarmed. 'Isn't that where people go to get a quickie divorce?' asked my second son.

'Yes,' I said, trying to look enigmatic and interesting. 'You're not getting divorced, are you?' he asked bluntly. 'No,' I said, 'we're going to an outdoor pursuits trade fair.' The children slouched away, muttering things like 'boring'.

I have brought my children up to be polite, but I fear that they are most impolite – under their breath. I call them children, but they are all grown-up. My eldest son has started to develop fine lines around his eyes – fledgling crow's-feet. A terrible sight for any parent to see.

There isn't a word for grown-up children, though I must admit 'groanies' comes instantly to mind. Are there parents out there who think that once their children reach the age of eighteen they are off your hands? Excuse me while I laugh, a cynical, dry, mirthless kind of laugh. I, too, thought as you did. Eighteen was the magical number in my mind as I endeavoured to pack my groceries at Sainsbury's, while one or more of my children had a spectacular tantrum under the trolley.

Anyway, this piece isn't about the damned groanies, it's about holidays. The first thing to be said about holidays is that anybody who can afford one should be grateful. The second thing is that planning holidays can be hard work. In my household it starts with somebody muttering: 'I suppose we ought to think about a holiday.' This remark is usually made in July and is received glumly, as if the person making it has said: 'I suppose we ought to think about the Bolivian balance of payments problem.'

Nothing much happens for a week and then the potential holiday-makers are rounded up and made to consult their diaries. Hospital appointments are taken into consideration, as are important things to do with work. But other highlights on the domestic calendar, such as the cat's birthday, are swept aside and eventually two weeks are found. The next decision is the most painful: where?

We travel abroad to work quite a lot but we return tired and weary, so the holiday we are planning is a slob's holiday: collapse on a sunbed, read a book until the sun goes down, stagger back to hotel room, shower, change into glad rags, eat well, drink well, wave goodbye to teenagers, have last drink on hotel terrace, go to bed then lie awake and wait for hotel waiters to bring teenagers home from disco.

I never want to be guided around another monument, as long as I live. I do not want to be told how many bricks it took to build the damned thing. I have a short attention span for such details.

I also want to live dangerously and get brown. I want to see my doughy English skin change from white sliced to wheat germ. I like the simple pleasure of removing my watch strap and gazing at the patch of virgin skin beneath.

I do not want to attend a 'folk evening' ever, ever again.

The kind where men with their trousers tucked into their socks wave handkerchiefs in the direction of women wearing puff-sleeved blouses, long skirts and headscarves.

I don't want to make new friends on holiday; I can't manage the ones I have at home. I do not want to mix with the locals and I have no wish to go into their homes. I do not welcome tourists who come to Leicester into my home. Why should the poor locals in Holidayland be expected to? Isn't it bad enough that we monopolize their beaches, clog their pavements and spend an hour in a shop choosing a sunhat that costs the equivalent of 75 pence?

So, the slob's holiday has several essential requirements: a hotel on a sandy beach, a balcony, good food, a warm sea, nightlife for the teenagers, a big crowd to get lost in, and an absence of mosquitoes. It's so tiring applying that repellent. I would also prefer it to be in a Muslim country where all the beautiful women are clad from head to toe in black. On this point my husband and I disagree.

As I write, we are still at the planning stage. We have looked through all the holiday brochures, but they are full of references to 'hospitable locals', 'folk nights', 'deserted beaches' and 'interesting historical sights'.

Not our cup of tea, or glass of sangria, at all. We slobs of the world must unite (if we can find the energy). We have nothing to lose, except our torpor.

My Vivienne Westwood
is Gone

When I was a child I was warned to keep away from the gypsies who used to set up a summer camp at the side of a little river in our neighbourhood.

I was an obedient child so I didn't actually go *inside* the traditional caravans and take tea with the gypsies, but I got as near as I could and became fascinated by their way of life. It seemed idyllic: the children ran free, they didn't have to go to school, they were allowed to ride bareback on their horses and ponies, and, by the look of things, they didn't have to wash or brush their hair in the mornings.

The adult gypsies seemed to enjoy life. The women washed their clothes in the river and hung them on the hedgerows to dry. I liked the idea of cooking on a campfire. I liked the gaudy clothes they wore.

On Coronation Day, I dressed up as a gypsy for the fancy dress competition. I wore a bandanna round my head on which my mother had sewn a dozen curtain rings. The rest of the costume was a strange hybrid of Romany Gypsy and Pearly Queen.

I carried a basket of clothes pegs and bashed like crazy

on a tambourine until an irritable adult told me to stop. I didn't win. There were enough gypsies in the competition to start up our own encampment.

The winner was my sister Barbara who was a most original and convincing doll in a box. When the judges came round she didn't bat her long eyelashes, not once. Though she's batted them a few times since.

So, I've always had a soft spot for gypsies. I've defended them from people who accuse them of despoiling the countryside.

But I have been writing about our decent British gypsies. Last week, in Barcelona, I encountered quite a different type.

I was sitting at a pavement café, I had just changed some money and had mucho pesetas. My beautiful Vivienne Westwood bag was between my feet (I knew that Barcelona was bag-snatch heaven). It had taken me three weeks to pluck up the courage to buy that bag. It was an oblong of black leather, with long shoulder straps and a beautiful gold interior.

Inside the bag were (note the past tense): a navy blue passport, an aeroplane ticket, a large A4 notepad, three credit cards, pens, mucho pesetas, a Swiss army knife, a cosmetic bag, a bottle of insulin and syringes, a tube of Ambre Solaire, a litre bottle of water (it was a big bag), photographs plus the usual debris that all the women I know have at the bottom of their bags – buttons, safety pins, tissues, eyebrow tweezers, spent matches, till receipts, a scrap of paper with the date of the parents' evening written on it, two Paracetamols in a blister pack and a twisted paperclip used for emergency manicures. As you must have guessed by now, the Barcelonian gypsies parted me from the bag and its contents.

Here's how they did it. They swooped on me. There were three fat women and two thin children. One woman pushed a distressed-looking carnation down my equally distressed-looking cleavage. The other women distracted my companions. I pulled the carnation out of the front of my T-shirt and handed it back to the woman. She pushed it back. The carnation went to and fro like Elizabeth Taylor's divorce lawyer.

Eventually the woman accepted the fact that I was not going to buy the withered carnation and she went away, but not before cursing me loudly and banging on the table.

My companions and I laughed until I went for my bag and found a sickening space between my feet.

The gypsies had been gone for at least five minutes. There was a pause and somebody said, 'Well they'll be celebrating around the campfire tonight.' It might even have been me.

I encountered such kindness from the Barcelona police I almost forgot that the last time I'd encountered them they had been clubbing a young man half to death with their batons.

In the unlikely event that those thieving raggled, taggled gypsies are reading this article, please remind me when it's the next parents' evening.

And in the more likely event that Vivienne Westwood is reading – I suggest that her next collection could be the gypsy look. They've already got the handbag.

Avoidance Activity

I am in Birmingham sitting in a café opposite a hairdresser's. I'm trying to find the courage to go in and book an appointment. I've been here three-quarters of an hour and I'm on my second large cappuccino. The table I'm sitting at has a wobble like a choirboy's Adam's apple. Consequently, I've spilt some of the first cup of coffee and most of the second down the white trousers I was so proud of as I swanked in front of the mirror in my hotel room this morning.

I can see the hairdressers, or stylists as they prefer to be called, as they work. There is a man with a ponytail who is perambulating around the salon, stopping now and then to frown and grab a hank of customer's hair. There are two girl stylists: one has had her white blonde hair shaved and then allowed it to explode into hundreds of hedgehog's quills; the other has hair any self-respecting woman would *scalp* for: thick and lustrous. All three are dressed in severe black. Even undertakers allow themselves to wear a little white at the neck and cuffs, but undertakers don't take their work half as seriously, and there lies the problem. I'm afraid of hairdressers.

When I sit in front of the salon mirror stuttering and blushing and saying that I don't quite know what I want, I know I am the client from hell. Nobody is going to win 'Stylist of the Year' with me as a model.

'Madam's hair is very th . . .'; they begin to say 'thin', think better of it and change it to 'fine' – ultimately, coming out with the hybrid word 'thine'. I have been told my hair is 'thine' many times. Are they taught to use it at college? Along with other conversational openings, depending on the season:

1 Done your Christmas shopping?
2 Going away for Easter?
3 Booked your summer holiday?
4 You're brown, been away?
5 Nights are drawing in, aren't they?
6 Going away for Christmas?

I'm hopeless at small talk (and big talk); I'm also averse to looking at my face in a mirror for an hour and a half. The result is that I sound evasive and look furtive. I behave as though I'm a prisoner on the run: James Cagney in lipstick and hooped earrings.

I've looked at wigs in stores, but I'm too shy to try them on, and I still remember the horror of watching a bewigged man jump into a swimming pool and then seeing what looked like the corpse of a medium-sized rodent break the surface and float brazenly on the water. He snatched at his wig, thrust it anyhow on top of his head and left the pool. I didn't see him for the rest of the holiday, perhaps he was skulking in his hotel room reliving the nightmare moment when he forgot the hair on his head was not his own, but had been purchased over a shop counter.

There is a behavioural trait that a lot of writers share – it is called avoidance activity. They will do anything to avoid starting to write: swig vodka, clean a drain, phone their senile uncle in Peru, change the cat's litter tray. I'm prone to this myself: in summer, I deadhead the flowers, even lobelia; in winter I'll keep a fire going, stick by stick, anything to put off the moment of scratching marks on virgin paper.

I'm indulging in avoidance activity right now. I've just ordered another cappuccino. I've tried giving myself a severe talking to: For God's sake woman! You're forty-seven years of age. Just cross the road, push the salon door open, and ask for an appointment!

It didn't work. I'm now in my hotel room, and have just given myself a do-it-yourself hairdo, which consisted of a shampoo, condition and trim, with the scissors on my Swiss army knife.

I can't wait to get back to the Toni & Guy salon in Leicester. The staff there haven't once called my hair 'thine' and they can do wonders with the savagery caused by Swiss army knife scissors.

This article is forty-nine words short and my brain has gone dead. To avoid writing, I took a pencil and obliterated the bags under my eyes, so evident in the picture in last month's Sainsbury's *The Magazine*. It would improve my self-esteem no end if you, kind reader, would do the same.

Control Freak? Moi?

I'm sitting on a plane at Edinburgh airport watching the luggage handlers at work. I'm fascinated by one man in particular. He is tall and has only half a head of hair. He has the lugubrious face of a natural comedian. In between throwing luggage into the hold he is afflicted by several minor inconveniences. A loose thread from his clothing wafts about, touching his face. He tries to grab at the thread, but he is wearing padded industrial gloves and so the thread continues to elude him. Then a fly lands on his chest. He brushes it off, it lands on his arm, his shoulder, his neck. The man curses, I can see his lips moving. He then starts to sneeze. I can't hear the sneeze because I am cocooned inside the plane, but I can tell from the way his body is jack-knifing that the sneezes are violent and noisy. During a lull in the sneezing the man pushes out a handkerchief, it falls to the ground and is blown away across the runway. He turns the conveyor belt off and chases the handkerchief. While his back is turned a red sports bag throws itself off the conveyor and rolls *under* the conveyor. The man catches up with his handkerchief, blows his nose vigorously and returns to his work.

I look down at the red sports bag. I am anxious now. Will the man notice it? Should I report it to somebody? I know there is a Scottish international football referee on the plane. Is the bag his? Does it contain the vital tools of his trade? The luggage man continues with his work, batting occasionally at the thread, the fly and now his hair because the wind has stiffened and his remaining hair is being blown forwards into his eyes.

I am willing the man to look down and see the red sports bag, but his attention is elsewhere. A colleague has joined him and they are now sharing a joke. My man bends double with laughter, then has a coughing fit. His colleague strolls away and my man swats at the invisible thread, the fly which has returned, and his intractable hair.

The pilot announces that final checks are being made and that we are due to depart within a few minutes. My man outside doesn't appear to know this. He has slowed down. He is rubbing the small of his back and grimacing. Now his bootlace has come undone, he stops the conveyor, puts his boot on the side and re-ties the lace. He takes his time and although the sports bag must be within his line of vision, he appears not to notice it. The pilot rambles on, talking about the weather in London. He tells us his name, which I immediately forget, but I do know that it is a reassuring name, something like Peter Worthington, David Morgan or Chris Parker. Good, solid names.

I'd put good money on it that they don't let you into pilot training college if you have a flashy, unreliable-sounding name. And, personally, I'd rather not have a Spike De Maurier at the controls as we encounter turbulence over the Alps. I know this is illogical and unfair, but as the plane falls out of the sky I want a Peter, a David or a Chris to tell me that 'We'll soon be passing through this small spot of bother'.

My man outside is in pain, not metaphysical pain, but physical. Every time he picks up a suitcase, he looks to be in agony. I've got some strong painkillers in my bag and I long to leave the plane and give him a couple (and at the same time to point out the damned red sports bag).

This article was going to be about our holiday in Cyprus where, yes, despite swearing never to again, we ended up watching the wretched folk dancing *and* wandering around ruins in temperatures similar to that of a space craft re-entering the earth's atmosphere. We also went to see Aphrodite's pool, where the Goddess was reputed to conduct her ablutions. It was not breathtakingly beautiful being surrounded by empty fag packets and faded Coke cans.

However, enough of that. How's our man doing with the luggage? There are now only three bags to load and the red sports bag is still there, unnoticed, under the conveyor. Shall I knock on my porthole window and try to alert my man? Me? A control freak? Never.

The Hilton Apron
Mystery

My sister Kate drove me down to Heathrow and I sat beside her putting the final touches to a film script. She parked outside International Departures, I wrote 'The End', handed the scruffy pages to her and ran inside to catch a plane to Australia. I had only a small bag and it was mostly full of crumpled, dirty clothes. When I arrived at my hotel, the Perth Hilton, I reached eagerly for the laundry list. I reproduce the list below. The prices are in Australian dollars, but the prices aren't what caused me to laugh out loud.

Dress	$ 13.50
Skirt	$ 8.50
Jacket	$ 10.50
Blouse	$ 8.00
Slacks	$ 8.50
Jeans	$ 8.50
Tracksuit	$ 15.50
Apron	$ 8.50
Woollens	$ 8.50

Did you spot it? *Apron*. What kind of woman is it who takes an apron to a five-star hotel? Picture the scene. This woman arrives at reception, she checks in, is given a key. A porter is summoned. He takes her bag, shows her to the lift, they chat. He leads the way to the room, opens the door, the woman gasps. The room is sumptuous; the bathroom is spotless; the towels are virgin white; and the marble surfaces sparkle. The porter shows her the minibar and opens the sliding doors. The woman steps on to the terrace and looks at the view. She then hands him a tip and he goes.

She puts her clothes away, then takes a bath, dries herself and wraps herself in the white bathrobe she finds behind the bathroom door. She fixes herself a gin and tonic, then makes several international telephone calls. The woman is talking to her employees, checking the fluctuations of various financial institutions.

After discussing a deal worth several million yen, she finds she has a couple of hours before her first business meeting with a Perth property developer. She goes on to the terrace and looks over at the land she intends to buy. It is on the bank of the Swan River; she intends to build a tasteful theme park there.

However, conscious that she is encroaching on a man's world, she looks at the aprons she has brought with her. All six are attractive but she selects the blue one with the fluffy kitten on the front. She puts it on then takes out a large toiletry bag. Inside is Mr Sheen, a duster, a scrubbing brush and a bottle of Windolene. The woman proceeds to clean the already immaculate room. Then, throwing the dirty apron into the laundry bag, she showers and dresses in her power suit, picks up her briefcase and goes out to buy herself a slice of Perth's redevelopment.

As she passes reception, the concierge hands her a sheath of faxes. She glances at them as she settles into the back seat of her hired limousine. Apparently there is a small apron factory for sale in the north of England. She picks up the car phone and speaks to Edgar Harbottle, the managing director of Feminine Aprons Ltd. After a brief negotiation she buys the company. Mr Harbottle says, 'I don't think you'll regret it, madam. Women will always need aprons, even in these post-feminist days.'

The woman is surprised at Mr Harbottle's grasp of sexual politics. He hadn't sounded like a man with such fine sensibilities. The driver of the limousine turns round and leers, 'I like to see my missis in an apron, at the sink; gets me all of a doo-da, know whaddi mean, Sheila?' He winks a horrible, salacious wink and the woman brusquely orders him to keep his eyes on the road, and tells him that her name is Eve, not Sheila. The democratic driver is not intimidated by the woman's refined English accent. 'Nah,' he says, 'women are all the same with a bag over their heads and wearing an apron.'

After a successful meeting the woman returns to her room, puts another apron on and cleans the bath and washbasin. She then throws this essential garment into the laundry bag and writes '2' in the box marked 'Apron'.

This story is, of course, a fantasy, but the Perth Hilton laundry list is fact. Explanations on a postcard, please.

Don't Become a Writer

Can anybody tell me why I want to work in the film industry? I recently finished the eleventh rewrite of a film, sent it off, heard nothing for three weeks, then had an enthusiastic phone call from Producer A – 'Very good.' To be followed three days later by an unenthusiastic phone call from Producer B – 'Needs more work.'

Who do I listen to, A or B? Is A lying? Does B secretly hate me? Will I be rewriting this film when my teeth are in a glass at the side of my bed and my Zimmer frame is within reach? Will the warden of my sheltered housing unit ask condescendingly, 'And when is this film you're writing going to be on our screens, Mrs Townsend?'

There is a trough of despair that most writers fall into at some stage. I'm in it now. My trough is the Grand Canyon. I fantasize about working in a biscuit factory, packing the Bourbon Creams, clocking in, clocking off and having a life. Do biscuit packers lie awake at night worrying about their work? Do they fret about the moment when the public tear away the packaging and see the Bourbon Creams nestling in their crinkly nests, next to the Vanilla Wafers and Ginger Nuts?

Do they imagine harsh criticism like, 'These Bourbon Creams are an utter disgrace; whoever packed these is a moron. I am writing to the manufacturers at once!'

Perhaps a few, but not many.

Many years ago I was asked by an American producer to go to Hollywood for six weeks. He wanted me to 'inject some humour' into an existing film script. I didn't get to read the script, because I didn't go. But I still have this image of myself lying by a pool with a bottle labelled 'Humour', using a hypodermic syringe and injecting humour into lines of dialogue. I imagined other writers with bottles labelled 'Pathos', 'Drama' and 'Structure', doing the same thing.

When I sit down to watch a film on television the room empties. My family scatter. I am a terrible viewer. I sneer, mock and swear at the screen. 'As if she'd do that!' I shout, as the heroine goes down the unlit cellar steps, straight into the arms of the axe murderer.

But in my heart of hearts, I know why the writer wrote that scene. The poor, demented creature was probably on the fifteenth rewrite and was by then incapable of thinking up anything more original. In fact only yesterday I wrote:

Scene 79. Interior. Cellar steps. Night.
Eleanor walks down the cellar steps carrying a candle. It goes out.

Which is bad enough. I haven't yet written:

Scene 90. Exterior. Dark alley. Night.
The villain's car speeds down the narrow alley. John Hero flattens himself against the wall. The car crashes into cardboard boxes, which seem to be brand new and empty.

Or even worse . . .

Scene 100. Interior. Empty warehouse. Day.
*The villain and John Hero run up and down stairs, creep about
and then have a fight for ten boring minutes.*

But I may be driven to it. In fact I can definitely feel a car
chase coming on, climaxing in a crash and a ball of flames.
Producers seem to like them. I know thousands of readers
would cut a limb off to see their unpublished articles, novels
and film scripts published and performed. Can I urge a little
caution? Before you buy the Jiffy bag and stamps and queue
up at the post office, take a moment to answer the following
questions:

a Do I want to be happy?
b Do I want my family to like me?
c Do I want to be described on hospital radio as 'our local
  scribbler'?
d Do I want to pay a literary agent 10 per cent of my income
  for the rest of my life?
e If successful, do I want to be loathed by other professional
  writers?
f If unsuccessful, do I want to be loathed by other professional
  writers?
g Do I want to see unflattering photographs of myself in the
  local paper?

If you have answered 'yes' to all these questions, then
you should go ahead and post your damn manuscript. But
don't come whining to me when you're rewriting your car
chase scene for the fifteenth time.

Christmas Presents Problems

I've just found a plastic bag hanging inside the cellar door. The bag's contents baffled me for a moment, and then I remembered Christmas Eve 1993, and the horrible memories came flooding back. Inside the bag were:

1. A replica of a Forties-style radio
2. A presentation box of sealing wax, ribbon and a seal-stamp engraved with the letter B
3. A pair of clip-on silver earrings
4. A pair of wide long-leg jeans, size 12
5. An opened bag of party poppers

Have you heard about the awful woman who does her Christmas shopping in the January sales? Does such an appalling woman exist, or is she an urban myth? Everybody seems to know one of these unnatural paragons, although nobody so far has confessed to being her.

I am seriously thinking of becoming her myself. I cannot take the strain of being a last-minute Christmas shopper ever again. And when I say last minute, that is exactly what I mean.

I was in W H Smith's at 5.30 p.m. on Christmas Eve when the tills were switched off, I was ushered towards the door and the lights went out. I staggered into the near-deserted shopping mall and sat on a bench muttering to myself, surrounded by a slithering mountain of shopping bags. I am surprised that a charity didn't offer me a bed for the night. A gang of drunken young men walked by and laughed at my hat. (When I got home and looked in the mirror I understood why – something peculiar had happened to the brim.)

I started Christmas shopping in November in New Zealand, so nobody can say I didn't try. I carted three very attractive throws back to England, together with a 4ft-long wooden Maori war canoe – but that's another story. I then went mad in a trinket shop in Covent Garden; how smug I must have sounded as I announced to the indifferent assistant, 'I'm doing my Christmas shopping early this year.'

How happy I was on the train going back to Leicester, as I gloated over the presents I'd bought, convinced that I'd got the Christmas shopping beast under control.

I compare the self-satisfied woman on the train in November to the pitiful wreck on the bench on Christmas Eve, and ask myself what went wrong. My family have various theories . . .

1 I'm a masochist; I enjoy the pain
2 I'm addicted to adrenalin
3 I'm a lazy slob
4 I'm a workaholic
5 I'm a drama queen
6 I'm the opposite of an anal retentive. Nobody knows the correct psychological term, but it's something disgusting, no doubt

As you may have noticed, I write lists compulsively, but as the days tick by towards Christmas Day, my lists become increasingly complicated. Do the children's presents add up to the same value? When wrapped, will they have the same satisfying bulk? Was one son serious about wanting a flying lesson for Christmas? Was the other son hinting or merely telling the truth when he informed me that his rock-climbing rope was frayed? Could I cast aside my feminist principles and buy a sewing machine for one daughter and a set of French ovenware for another?

On Christmas Eve 1993 I forgot every principle I've ever held: at around 4.30 p.m. I stood in a queue in Woolworth's, holding two bridal Barbie dolls and two pairs of toddler-size Mr Blobby socks. I can only plead temporary insanity, and report that on Christmas Day my granddaughters both stripped Barbie of her wedding frock, saying they preferred her in the nude. I suspect that the Mr Blobby socks have been pushed to the back of a drawer.

It was a traditional sort of Christmas Day: the record tokens were thrown away with the rubbish, the grand-children played all day with the cheapest present (Plasticine) and the roast potatoes wouldn't brown, but I had been deeply scarred by the last-minute shopping.

Dad If you're reading this, the replica Forties radio was meant for you. It was made in Taiwan and after I put in the batteries that's all I could hear: Taiwanese. That's why you ended up with the book tokens.

Barbara The silver clip earrings refused to clip on to anything.

Husband What would you have done with the sealing wax and ribbon?

The wide-leg jeans I bought for myself – a mistake. I look

like Charlie Chaplin in them, but I've lost the receipt. The party poppers were faulty: when the strings were pulled, something like multi-coloured cat litter covered the kitchen floor.

Janet and John

I was eight years old before I could read. My teacher was a despot. I will call her Mrs X. (She died long ago, but I am still afraid of her.) Her method of teaching reading was to give every child in the class a copy of *Janet and John* and have us point to each word, then chant it aloud. The stories in *Janet and John* were not exactly riveting. Daddy would go off in the morning, wearing his trilby, overcoat and gloves, carrying a strange bag which I now know to be a briefcase. Daddy always wore the same clothes, even in summer. Mummy would wave him goodbye. She usually wore a pretty frock, frilly apron and high heels. If she went shopping in the village she changed into a nifty suit, a felt hat and gloves, of course.

Janet and John seemed to live in the garden. They got on remarkably well, unlike most brothers and sisters I know. They had a nice, cheeky-faced dog called Spot, and they spent a lot of time shouting, 'Look, Spot, look! Look at the ball! Fetch the ball!'

When Daddy came home from work he would take off his overcoat and hat, stick a pipe between his manly teeth, sit down in a big square armchair and read the newspaper. Through the open kitchen door Mummy could be seen, smiling serenely as she prepared tea. She would then go to the kitchen door and shout, 'Come here, Janet! Come here, John!' And Janet and John would climb down the tree, or get out of the boat (they seemed to have a river at the bottom of their garden) and Mummy and Daddy and Janet and John would have their scrumptious tea: sandwiches, jam tarts and jelly.

The table was draped with a white tablecloth, and sometimes Spot could be seen grinning cheekily from beneath it. Mummy and Daddy occasionally went into the garden, where the sun always shone, and the flowers behaved themselves and grew in perfect rows. Daddy would push the lawnmower and Mummy would hang out the washing. There was never underwear on Mummy's clothes line, but there was always a good drying wind that made the wet clothes billow and flap. Daddy's hair was never ruffled by the wind; he was a devotee of Brilliantine. In the evening, when Janet and John were in bed, Mummy and Daddy sat in a pool of light under their respective standard lamps. Mummy darned socks and Daddy smoked his pipe and did the crossword.

There is a good chance that John Major was taught to read from the *Janet and John* books. I strongly suspect that when he introduced the phrase 'Back to basics' it was their ideal ordered world he had at the back of his mind. But I have found an uncensored copy of *Janet and John* and it makes distressing reading.

Janet and John Go into Care. Daddy is getting ready for work. 'Where are my gloves, Mummy?' he asks. 'Look, Daddy, look, there are your gloves,' snaps Mummy, 'though why you should want to wear gloves in August defeats me!'

Spot runs in and knocks Daddy's briefcase over. A copy of *Health and Efficiency* slithers out and falls open at a picture of nudists playing tennis. John runs in, 'Look, Janet, look!' Daddy hits John on the head with his pipe, kicks Spot and leaves for work. Mummy dries her tears and walks to the village shop. She is still upset by the row with Daddy and she slips a tin of corned beef into her wicker basket.

Mummy is arrested for shoplifting. When Janet and John arrive home from school, Mummy isn't there. The front door is locked; they sit on the doorstep and wait. It starts to rain. 'Look, John, look!' says Janet eventually. 'There is Mummy.' John looks up and sees Mummy in the back of a police car.

John and Janet put Mummy to bed; she asks them to prepare their own tea. They put the kettle on the stove, then go out to play in their boat on the river. It is getting dark when they return.

'Look, Janet, look!' John is pointing to a red glow in the sky. A social worker is on the river bank. She breaks the news gently. The house has burned down, their father has run away with a woman who owns a glove shop, and their mother has been taken to the cottage hospital with shock. 'Look, Janet, look!' says John. 'We're back to basics.'

Backbone

Hello back sufferers everywhere. I've joined the club. There is a new entry in my telephone book under C – for chiropractor. Fate struck me down the day before The First Night of my new play, *The Queen and I*.

Six months of bad-postured writing, which included crouching over dimly lit hotel dressing tables and scribbling on juddering Intercity 125 trains, collided with the contained hysteria of the rehearsal room. As it became clear that the play I had written would need a massive rewrite, the result of this physical and emotional collision could easily have been a nervous breakdown.

Writers are prone to going barmy, but fate decided to strike me down in quite a different way. It put me on my back by messing about with three discs and allowing one to slip out. I don't blame the disc – for forty-eight years it had been in the same place, at the bottom of my spine, doing its job uncomplainingly. Who can blame it for slipping out for a look around? But it could have chosen a dull patch to go, instead of the day of The First Night. Something had to be done – my sisters took me to a chiropractor.

I looked like a human question mark. Bent, but not curious. Pain takes the curiosity away. Pain is introspective, it doesn't give a damn about the rest of the world, it concentrates on itself. Through gritted teeth, I explained that I had to attend The First Night. The chiropractor took x-rays of my spine and me: two worn discs and one that had gone absent without leave. He advised immediate bed rest. 'Impossible!' I said. I expect there was a note of hysteria in my voice. It is not as if I like First Nights – who does? The prospect of being in an auditorium with 700 people and watching them fail to laugh at your jokes is a refined form of torture. I once went to see a play of mine with seven companions, and four of them fell asleep. One of them was my husband. But, horrible as First Nights are, they have a compulsion. I know of no playwright who does not attend. Some stand at the back of the theatre in the dark. Some get drunk in the bar, some wander the streets nearby, and some, believe it or not, actually sit in the stalls, surrounded by their critics!

I managed to convince my bone manipulator that, if necessary, I would crawl to the theatre that night, and he graciously capitulated and took a passion-killing, flesh-pink support belt out of a drawer and wrapped it around me. My sisters took me home to bed, where I stayed until it was time to don the black velvet frock and the black velvet high heels. I staggered crab-like into the theatre and propped myself up against a stair rail. When the audience had filed in, looking excited and eager (poor deluded fools), I lay on my back on the seats in the foyer and listened to the bar staff assembling the interval drinks for the guests and critics. 'A heavy-drinking lot – put out more bottles,' said the manager, after casting a professional eye over the audience.

Two minutes before the interval, I asked a passing barman called Barry to haul me to my feet and I stood propped up against a wall, waiting for the audience to burst out of the auditorium and make its usual frantic dash to the bar. I prepared myself for the worst: that of overhearing strangers making unkind comments about the play. I didn't hear one. People were talking about the weather, Bosnia and the price of turnips, as they tend to do in the interval. After all, there is another act to be sat through, the jury is still out. My family told me that they had laughed themselves stupid, but it takes very little to make them laugh; they used to have hysterics at the sight of Paul Daniels's toupee.

I crawled up the stairs to the balcony to see the last scene. I watched on my knees as the cast of nine wonderful actors took their bows. I noted bitterly that the two puppets (for whom I'd written no lines) got the warmest applause. I then adjusted my surgical support belt and geared myself for the verdict of the audience.

You need backbone to work in the theatre.

The Craft Fayre

'**Never, never take** me to a craft fair again, even if I beg
and scream and implore you, do you promise?'

'I promise,' said my husband, gripping the steering wheel
with barely concealed rage as we joined a queue of cars leaving the craft fair car park. At my insistence we had broken a
cardinal rule: never leave the house on a bank holiday.

Some long-repressed herding instinct had swept over me
the night before and I had pored over the *Leicester Mercury*,
looking for local attractions to visit. 'Aha,' I cried eventually,
and began to sell the idea of visiting a country house,
complete with woodland walks, market garden and craft
fair, to my husband. I had been in a peculiar mood all week,
beset with doubts and insecurities, dithering at the wardrobe
door in the morning, etc. So, no doubt as a way of appeasing
the madwoman, my husband agreed to leave the house on
a bank holiday. It was a glorious afternoon, we shouted
goodbye to the teenage daughter who was skulking in her
room, hiding from the sun, and joined the bank holiday
traffic. We tootled along happily, listening to *The Archers* on
Radio 4.

As we listened to the afternoon play (a modern drama about family life, involving incest, murder and madness), the first signs started to appear on fluorescent cardboard tied to lampposts: 'Craft Fayre'. Of course we should have turned back there and then, done a Starsky and Hutch three-point turn and headed for home at full speed. To spell fair as fayre is ten out of ten naff. It is as bad as calling a café Ye Olde Tea Shoppe or a cart selling sweets Ye Olde Sweet Kabin.

I saw the latter in a city centre shopping mall last week. To confuse the issue, the boy weighing the pick'n'mix wore an old-fashioned butcher's uniform, complete with striped apron and straw boater. Ludicrous when you think that the sweets are probably made by machinery in a business unit on a windswept industrial estate.

But, patient reader, we did not turn back. Like lemmings, knowing our fate but unable to control it, we rushed towards the edge of the cliff. I shuffled my credit cards impatiently as we approached the grounds of the country house. I counted my cash as we joined a long queue of traffic. I could hardly stop myself from leaping out of the car as we toured the various car parks looking for a space. Eventually, my husband bumped up the car's suspension and drove down a rutted cart track, parked in a ditch, and at last we were able to join the madding bank holiday crowds.

'Tea Rooms', it had said in the newspaper, and I conjured up images of plump apple-cheeked waitresses serving home-made scones warm from the oven. The tea rooms had a long queue, which my husband gallantly joined, leaving me to sit outside in the sunshine. I was perfectly happy for the first half hour. Then I began to be concerned. Had he fallen into a black hole or had he gone berserk and smashed the tea rooms to smithereens in a frenzy of impatience and hunger? Eventually he emerged carrying a tray, on which lurked two sad scones. At a glance I could tell that these apologies had only recently made the journey from freezer to microwave to cash till. There were no apple-cheeked waitresses, either – just one gawky teenage girl who looked to be in need of orthodontic treatment. With globs of scone sticking to our palates, we entered the craft workshops.

I wasn't aware that sticking nuts and bolts together and making little men sitting astride nut and bolt motorcycles had ever called for a seven-year craft apprenticeship. I was not tempted by the clumsy jewellery made from polished beach pebbles, or by the machine-made quilts in insipid colours. As for the New Age Merlin wall plaques, they looked like solidified cat poo. I almost broke a hundred crystals in my rush to get out of that particular shop. The pottery was heavy and dull and slime green. You wouldn't want it on your table, though it could have been handy for slitting your wrists over as you crawled home, bumper to bumper, in the bank holiday traffic.

Missing Husband

I have lost thousands of things over the years: umbrellas, gloves, handbags, diaries, jackets, cats, etc. I once left my baby son parked outside the Co-op in his royal family-style pram and strolled home without him. It was his first outing and he slept throughout. So I admit to being somewhat absent-minded, but I'm working on it. I have three note-books on the go at the moment – the problem is that I've lost two of them. I know that they're in the house somewhere. One of them contains the article that I am trying to re-present here.

Four weeks ago I lost my husband – he was on one Greek island and I was on another. A mad travel agent had sent him to Thessalonika on the mainland, which is the equivalent of a Greek wishing to go to London being sent via the Outer Hebrides. The travel agent's madness did not stop there; he told my husband that the ferry services to Skyros were so frequent that a timetable was not necessary. The 'so frequent' turned out to be one a week on Mondays. My husband found this out on Friday morning. Our arrangement had been that I would meet the first ferry from

Thessalonika on Friday morning. On Thursday night, I knew the awful truth, but I still felt compelled to go to Linaria, the little harbour on Skyros, to meet the boat and the phantom husband.

Elias drove me in his Mercedes taxi; he has a degree in English from Athens University. He and I were to become closely bonded over the next two days. He once had Jeffrey Archer in the back of his cab. Apparently, Lord Archer has a penchant for the ceramics of Skyros, and after disembarking from a yacht in the harbour proceeded to plunder the shops. Elias told me that the famous literary lord announced, 'I am Jeffrey Archer,' as he climbed into the cab. Elias replied, 'I do not know you.' I asked him what impression Lord Archer had made on him. 'His wife is very nice,' said Elias diplomatically.

It was not possible to communicate with my husband, but I know him to be a resourceful man, not the type to twiddle his thumbs at Thessalonika harbour until Monday. I knew he would work out a route to Skyros. There were several options: plane, ferry and flying dolphin – a sort of hydrofoil on skis. It became clear that every plane, ferry and flying dolphin would have to be met. Elias pledged his support and he and I drove from one side of the island to the other. The airport consists of a Portakabin, the plane looked like something out of an aeronautical museum, and it carried only nineteen people. As the last white knobbly-kneed Englishman appeared on the aeroplane steps, I would shake my head and Elias would rev up the Merc and we would speed towards the harbour.

I became an object of pity; old women in black would enquire after my health and spirits. The taverna owner opposite the ferry docking point would shake his head in sympathy. Meanwhile, ferries and flying dolphins came and went, husbandless. Elias made a joke once – 'Perhaps he will never come.' I laughed, but it wasn't hearty laughter. Then one morning, after meeting one plane, one ferry and one flying dolphin, Elias said, 'Sue, in five minutes you will see your husband.' And he was right – a flying dolphin drew up and there he was, blowing kisses through the cabin window. Elias withdrew ten yards and watched as my husband and I were reunited on the quay. If it had been a film, the old woman in black, the taverna owner and the fishermen would have cheered and carried my husband shoulder-high to the taverna – but this was real life, so they didn't. But I think they were quietly pleased.

During the week we spent on Skyros, my husband was approached many times by people sympathizing with his travel difficulties. 'I quite enjoyed it,' he would reply. 'It was an adventure.' Which made me wonder about Elias' other joke – the one about the beautiful young Greek girl at Thessalonika.

Mary the Doll

I've got a doll called Mary. She sits on a bookshelf in my workroom (where I do no work), wearing a knitted vest and knicker outfit and a hideous purple crocheted dress. She is made of pot (or bisque if you want to be posh) and her limbs and head are fastened to her torso by elastic bands. Her face is prettily painted, and the reason she sits high up on the bookshelf is that I like her very much and I am determined to keep her from harm.

My grandchildren are only allowed to hold her under strict adult supervision (mine). No religious ceremony can be as sombre as the moment I lift Mary from the shelf and place her into a grandchild's arms. The rules are that the child has to remain sitting and the doll has to remain dressed. As soon as my grandchildren could speak, I told them that Mary had been my doll when I was a little girl, and I banged on about how carefully I had looked after my fragile doll. I probably had a horrible self-congratulatory smirk on my face as I did so.

A month ago I was placing the *Observer* business supplement on the floor against my flooding dishwasher, when

I had a sudden memory flashback and saw myself walking into a junk shop in the inner city and buying Mary. I would have been thirty-five at the time. I went weak at the knees, which was quite convenient because I was soon on my knees trying to stem the sudsy flood from the dishwasher. How could I have imagined and then recounted the story that I had known Mary for forty-eight years? As I paddled around the kitchen (incidentally, does anybody know a decent dishwasher mechanic in the Leicester area?), as I mopped and squeezed, I wondered what else I'd imagined. Was I truly the only child to fail the cycling proficiency test in my class at junior school? Was it really me who brought shame to the school open day by getting the ribbons tangled during the maypole dance? Perhaps it wasn't me who shouted 'Mackeson!' as the swan fluttered to her death during a school trip to see *Swan Lake* (Mackeson was being advertised for its reviving qualities at the time). Had I only imagined myself to be this clumsy, irreverent child? I put my brain into computer mode and tried to filter out more false memories.

I confessed to the first child who came to the house. 'Don't worry about it, Mum,' he said, with that tolerant smile people use when they talk to the simple-minded. The youngest daughter was less tolerant: 'You do it all the time,' she said, rolling her eyes about. The eldest daughter dropped another bombshell: 'You didn't buy Mary from a junk shop,' she said. 'You found her in a skip.'

I reeled about a bit, clutched my head, etc. How could I have deceived myself twice? I prayed that I wouldn't be called as a witness in a trial. I, who could no longer tell fact from fiction.

But I'm in good company. There was the famous case of

the Los Angeles Police Conference . . . or it could have been the New York Police, or was it San Francisco? Anyway, they had convened to talk about the reliability of witness evidence. An eminent doctor or psychologist or senior police person was halfway through a lecture when somebody wearing a gorilla outfit ran from the back of the hall up to the podium, pointed a banana (I think) at the lecturer, shouted 'Bang! Bang! Bang!' and ran out again. The lecturer ordered the police people in the hall immediately to write down what they'd seen, and out of 300 or 400 or 500 police people in the hall, not one of them got it right. (One person wrote that the gorilla was wearing a white tuxedo and was carrying a bunch of flowers.) It does make you question historical 'facts'. Was it cakes King Alfred burnt, or did he set his shoes alight whilst drying them next to the fire?

For years I've congratulated myself on my superior powers of observation, yacked on about the importance of 'truth' to anybody who would listen. But Mary has changed all that. Last night I allowed Doogie, my three-and-a-half-year-old granddaughter, to walk across my workroom with Mary in her arms.

PS. The dishwasher mechanic doesn't have to be 'decent'. I don't care what his or her morals are. I just want my dishwasher mended.

Book Early to Avoid Disappointment

Do you know how to have a bargain holiday, filled with mystery and the unexpected? I do. You rush into a travel agent's office on the Wednesday and you gabble that you want to be on a beach in Majorca on the Friday. The travel agent turns to her computer (usually with a sigh) and presses a few knobs. An hour later you leave the shop. You had stressed that you wanted to fly from East Midlands airport on the Friday, but you find yourself agreeing to fly from Gatwick on a late flight that will deposit you at Palma Airport at five minutes past five on the Saturday morning. You know that at that time all the babies on the plane will be wailing piteously, and that every child under five years old will be having mega tantrums by the luggage carousel (together with most of the adult men who will be brandishing their luggage trolleys like jousting knights of old).

We last-minute, bargain-holiday buyers are punished for our insouciance. We are not told where we are going to stay until just before we get on the coach. Along with our fellow travellers, we cluster around our holiday firm's representative, who is usually called Julie. The snaggletoothed couple from Wolverhampton at the front are given a hotel voucher. 'The Splendide,' says Julie, and you know by her awed tone of voice that the Hotel Splendide is where the King of Spain stays when his villa is being redecorated. The next voucher is given to the large family of Eastenders who had surrounded you on the plane. Julie says, 'The Bon Vista Apartments, on the beach.' The voucher is handed over with a smile and received with smiles.

Then it is your turn. Julie cannot quite look you in the eye. 'Ah,' she says, on hearing your name. She mumbles something. It sounds like the Hellhole Hotel. You ask her to repeat it. It is the Hellhole Hotel. It is there written in Julie's childlike script, on the voucher. As you get on the coach you laugh with your partner and say brave things like 'Hellhole must mean something else in Spanish, or perhaps it has been misspelt. Hela Hola, for instance.'

The coach speeds through the Majorcan countryside while Julie runs through her spiel on a malfunctioning hand-held microphone. The 'scenery', as Julie calls it, is becoming visible in the grey dawn light. Julie suggests an outing. She tells us to go to Palma harbour and to pose beside a multi-millionaire's yacht and get somebody to take our photograph, then on our return home pretend the yacht was ours! She then suggests we visit Dias during our stay because Michael Douglas has a house there and we might 'rub shoulders with him in the grocery shop'. Eventually, the snaggle-tooths are dropped off at the truly splendid 'Splendide'. The Eastenders are deposited at the beachside apartments. By now the sun is up and the sea can be seen, brochure blue.

The coach is empty apart from you and your partner, Julie and the driver. The coach turns down a track and bumps along the potholes until it comes to a halt outside a building with so much peeling white stucco it looks like an incompetently iced wedding cake. A mangy dog is lying on the steps doing something disgusting with its tongue. But later, as you inspect your room and en-suite bathroom, you realize the dog was at least making an effort to clean itself. Which is something the hotel has failed to do to your room. You open the warped shutters and go out on to the balcony. The sea is nowhere to be seen.

You should book well ahead, I can hear you say. My sister booked a holiday in February for nine people, only to be told in July, at Dover (one hour before the ferry sailed), that she couldn't have the holiday she had booked and paid for because her hotel had been double-booked. After much trailing around various resorts, the nine ended up crammed into two rooms (my sister slept on the balcony). We are sure the company concerned will do the decent thing and compensate the nine people who had saved up all year and then been denied their holiday, and we are convinced the delay so far has been caused by an administrative error. There can surely be no other explanation. Can there?

Gimme Food and Newspapers

Another deadline, another rewrite, another hotel room. Blackpool this time. My room faces the sea and I sit and watch the tide come in and go out. There is an A4 pad on my knees and an inky pen in my hand, but not a single creative thought in my head.

I am rewriting a film, or rather I am failing to rewrite a film. I've lost count of the drafts I've written over the past four years. I think it's eight, but it could be nine. I think constantly about *Four Weddings and a Funeral* and screenwriter Richard Curtis. Mr Curtis wrote seventeen drafts, but this knowledge fails to comfort me.

I wish there was a big meaty part in my film for the star of *Four Weddings and a Funeral*, Hugh Grant, but there isn't. My male lead is a forty-five-year-old tortoise-fancier who is disgusted by sex and cuts his own hair – hardly Mr Grant's style.

I get up and pace around my room. I'm feeling slightly claustrophobic because I've only just vacated the suite down the corridor. Two friends came for the weekend and the suite worked out cheaper than booking three rooms.

'This is where Mrs Thatcher and John Major stay when they visit Blackpool,' said the charming Mr Price as he opened the door of the Westminster Suite. I had a sudden vision of Mrs Thatcher and John Major strolling along the Golden Mile, arm in arm, wearing Mr Blobby baseball caps. Had I fallen upon a scandal that would bring down the government? Unfortunately not. Apparently, it was strictly Margaret 'n' Denis and John 'n' Norma.

So, after the spacious glories of the suite in which there were four rooms to pace (five including the shower), I am reduced to the confined pacing of a tiger in a politically incorrect zoo.

Unless breakfast is included, I never eat in English hotels. I will eat at transport cafés, at caravans in lay-bys, but never in hotels. I suspect that the ingredients that go into hotel kitchens are marked 'Unfit for human consumption. Hotel use only'.

Whilst in Blackpool, I ate in Harry Ramsden's fish and chip emporium four times. I hate queuing, but the thought of that succulent fresh haddock inside that light crispy batter had me standing in line. (By the way, Harry, please do something about those two sets of doors. Trying to get a wheelchair through them is like trying to get Lady Olga Maitland a place in heaven.)

The fourth time I was accompanied by my parents and my sister, who had come to give me a lift back to Leicester. 'Didn't tek you long,' said our young waiter, looking down admiringly at our clean plates. We don't mess about with food in our family. We could speed-eat for England. Is it in the genes, or is it a primeval fear that our food is going to be snatched away from us?

Incidentally, has anyone ever finished a 'Harry's Challenge'? I saw a few foolhardy blokes order it from the menu, only to see their jaws drop when it was put before them. A 'Harry's Challenge' consists of a piece of haddock the size of a small child, surrounded by a pile of chips the height of a minor Welsh mountain. A lake of mushy peas sets it off nicely. Nobody I saw rose to the challenge.

Back at the hotel, I gloom out of the window at the sea, count the seagulls, watch the horizon for ships, paint my toenails cyclamen pink, and think until my head hurts. I allow myself no distractions; there are no books in my room, no magazines, and I don't turn the television on. However, the hotel pushes a complimentary copy of the *Daily Telegraph* under my door every morning. I must admit that my lip curled the first time I saw it lying there. We all have our prejudices, and one of mine was that the *Daily Telegraph* was read only by crusty old colonels with politics to the right of Genghis Khan. It's no secret that my politics are to the left of Lenin and Livingstone, so it came as a shock to find that I was actually enjoying the *Daily Telegraph*. It made me laugh, it was well written and it was critical of the present government.

I still have the *Guardian* delivered, but I now sneak out and buy the *Daily Telegraph for pleasure*. What next? Will I start foxhunting, wearing pussy-bow blouses or calling for capital punishment in schools? Watch this space.

Mugging

An elderly lady, Mrs Coleman, was mugged outside our house last week. She is seventy-five and was on her way to the hairdresser's. It was a beautiful day, the sort of day when you feel glad to be alive. Her husband was not feeling well, so she insisted that he stay at home instead of driving her to have her hair done, as he usually did.

My eldest daughter heard her shouting for help, looked out of the window and saw Mrs Coleman being helped to her feet by a female motorist and a neighbour from down the road. Together they brought Mrs Coleman into our house. She was covered in blood, her stockings were torn and she was holding the broken straps of her handbag in one hand. She was in extreme shock and was trembling uncontrollably. When she saw her reflection in the hall mirror she started to cry.

The police and an ambulance were sent for. A police motorcyclist came within minutes, others followed. Mrs Coleman managed to give a policeman who turned up in a patrol car a description of the assailant: white, young, on a bike, dark hair. The motorcyclist was despatched to try to find this cruel young man. The ambulancemen arrived and were kind and attentive to Mrs Coleman.

'We must tell your husband,' they said. Mrs Coleman became distressed. 'No,' she said, 'he's not well, he mustn't have a shock.' At this point my daughter had to leave the room, she was so upset and angry. Outside she found the police motorcyclist kicking at our garden wall in his frustration. The young man had vanished, and there were no eye-witnesses to the attack.

Mrs Coleman was carried, on a stretcher, from the house and taken to hospital. A policeman left to break the shocking news to Mr Coleman, and three of my children were left to talk about what they would like to do to the cowardly young man who had attacked a frail seventy-five-year-old woman.

We later found out that Mrs Coleman had a regular appointment at the hospital. She was undergoing a daily course of chemotherapy there. I felt a murderous rage when I arrived home and heard this sad story. I knew that Mrs Coleman's life would never be the same. I hoped it wouldn't stop her from walking down a pleasant tree-lined street on a lovely day in the middle of the afternoon again. But I guessed that it would probably diminish her life in many such small ways.

It is easy to despair of human nature at times like these. The temptation is to lock ourselves away from the world, to trust nobody and never venture out after dark. But if we do this the criminals have won. They will not only have taken away our money and our belongings, they will have snatched away our confidence and our freedom. It is important to remember that the dark-haired young man on the bicycle is in a tiny minority. Other criminals despise his type of cowardly crime, and, when he is eventually caught and sent to prison, his life will be made extremely uncomfortable. In the prison hierarchy he will be the lowest of the low, on a par with those convicted of crimes involving cruelty to children.

The overwhelming majority of people are law abiding and respectful of the need to protect and care for the very young and the very old. Most of us keep these moral laws automatically, which is why we are so outraged when one of our fellow human beings dares to break this moral code.

As I have said earlier, I wasn't at home at the time of Mrs Coleman's attack. I was in London attending the rehearsals of *The Queen and I*, which was due to open in the West End. So I was startled to read in the local paper that it was I who found Mrs Coleman in the street and brought her into the house.

For a moment I thought that I had finally lost all my marbles – that I had hallucinated the train journey to London, the rehearsals and the train journey back. I didn't understand how anybody could confuse my daughter with me: she is young and beautiful, and I am lateish middle-aged and, well, not beautiful.

Mrs Coleman gave a very spirited account of her attack to the local paper; she was speaking from her son's home where she was recovering from her injuries. I detected from what she said that she was a brave woman who was most indignant that a cruel stranger had entered her life and turned it upside down. And, now that I think about it, there may be a chance that she will walk down our road again in the afternoon. If she does, I hope she calls in for a cup of tea. I'd like to meet her, for real this time.

Prince Charles for King?

I've had this theory for some time. I've kept it to myself so far because I fear public ridicule. I feel like the person who, many hundreds of years ago, first ventured the opinion, 'Er, do you think it might be possible that er . . . the earth is . . . er, actually *round* instead of er . . . *flat*?' So bear with me, will you?

My theory is this: I think Prince Charles would be relieved if the institution of the monarchy was to be brought to an end. I have no evidence to put before you; I am certainly not on intimate terms with Prince Charles. In fact I am not on any terms with him. Nor am I likely to be. But I have this feeling.

On the face of it the job of king looks quite attractive. The money is extremely good, the holidays are long, you get to see the world, you don't have to worry about missing your plane because of roadworks on the M25 – your plane waits for you. Come to think of it, if you are king, what are you doing on the M25? Why aren't you in your own helicopter, flying above the traffic-bound masses?

When a king reaches his destination he doesn't have to

lug his baggage under a scorching sun towards a taxi driver who is picking his nose and wiping his finger on the upholstery. No, a king is led by flunkies towards an air-conditioned limousine that proceeds to drive along streets closed to normal traffic due to 'security'. There may be a little light waving to be done to the gaggles of flag-brandishing schoolchildren fainting of sunstroke on the pavement, but there is no danger of straining the royal wrist: for just as children from ordinary backgrounds are trained by their parents to open the top of a cornflakes packet without mangling the whole box, or to empty a pedal bin without scattering eggshells underfoot en route to the dustbin, so are royal children trained, almost from birth, to perfect their wave to the crowd.

Other advantages of being king are . . . meeting world-famous figures; having twenty-four hour room service (every day); and having a book written about you with a cover photograph that depicts you as being a deeply serious, anguished individual. Already bowed down with their future responsibilities, kings are able to leave home knowing that somebody will feed the pets and that the video won't be stolen. They don't lie awake at night worrying about class, agonizing, 'Am I upper-lower-middle?' or 'Am I lower-working scum?' Kings can confidently assert, 'I am upper, upper, upper' and know that no British person will contradict them.

When we wore lizardskin shoes and lived in caves, I suppose it made sense to have a king, somebody who bossed us about and made sure the fire was kept going.

In medieval times we were told that the king had been ordained by God and that a touch of his royal digit would cure us of our disgusting, scrofulous diseases. We also believed that the earth was flat and that mangel-wurzels were delicious. In other words, we were ignorant peasants who lived in hovels and did not have the advantage of public libraries. It's hard to be king in the late twentieth century. The public is so much more sophisticated. Babies are now born knowing how to programme the video to record *Rosie and Jim*.

Let us now look at the disadvantages of being king:

Travel You are met off the plane by a collection of late-middle-aged men in new suits, who sweat with nervous tension as they are introduced to you. Their handshakes feel like decomposing fish. They are nervous *because you are the king*.

Meeting the famous Most famous people are boring. They only want to talk about themselves and constantly interrupt when you want to talk about yourself. The only reason they agree to meet you is *because you are the king*.

Your biography Because your biographer comes from that ancient dynastic family the Dimblebys, you feel obliged to tell him all your innermost thoughts on the deprivations of your miserable childhood. You forget that your mother and father can read and that a good thrashing, a cold bedroom and poor food constituted the childhood of most British people born in the Forties. So you fail to get any sympathy and in your heart you know that the book has been commissioned, written and published *because they think you will be king*.

One day you say to yourself, 'I have not been ordained by God. I am human and I want to be *free*.'

Like I said, it's only a theory.

The Coat

There is a Chinese proverb. 'Beware of occasions that demand new clothes.' I consistently ignore this advice. On the occasion of my first American book promotion – a landmark in any writer's life – I not only ignored the advice, I laughed in its face.

I was walking down a street in London when I saw The Coat in a shop window. It was ankle length, suede and lined in sheepskin. I saw myself wearing it, in New York, in a snow storm. In my fantasy I was swapping witticisms with sophisticated New York publishers while we were entering a smart restaurant to celebrate the huge success of my book.

I went into the shop and touched The Coat. The suede was as soft as a lover's skin. A smiling girl murmured encouraging words and I soon found myself wearing The Coat and poncing up and down in front of what seemed like a particularly flattering mirror. The coat weighed nothing. I could have been wearing thistledown. The girl adjusted the collar so that it framed my face. I saw myself on the top of the Empire State Building, as snug as a bug despite the biting east wind blowing from the Hudson River.

Perhaps at this point I should inform you that the itinerary for my American tour was as follows: Heathrow – New York – Boston – New York – Washington – Miami – Heathrow.

Did you spot the odd one out? Miami boasts temperatures in the high nineties for most of the year, except for a couple of months when it drops to the high seventies. But, as I stood in the shop clad from ears to ankles in the dream coat, I banished Miami from what was left of my mind. The salesgirl (who had probably just graduated from the Royal Academy of Dramatic Art) said, 'I've been longing for somebody elegant and sophisticated to buy that coat.' Now, reader, in normal circumstances I would have laughed, because I know I am not elegant. My chipped nail varnish is legendary, my tights spring holes as soon as I take them out of the packet, and my black tailored suits are usually decorated with an inelegant sprinkling of white cat hairs. But the circumstances were not normal. I was going to four American cities where I would be giving readings from my book. I was terrified. So I chose to believe the salesgirl. She was obviously a great judge of character, I decided, and anyway I needed The Coat. It would protect me from hostile elements: the public and the weather.

I bought it. The price of The Coat is a secret I will take to my grave. My daughters, who take an almost obsessive interest in the price I pay for my clothes, put me through their usual KGB interrogation routine, but I did not crack.

The Coat was too long for any wardrobe in the house and it dragged on the floor of the cloakroom, so I hung it on a hanger from the picture rail in the hall. Visitors and family took to stroking it as though it were an exotic pet. The weather in England was unseasonably warm so I had yet to wear The Coat, but New York and that snow storm were never far from my mind.

There was a minor disaster when the dry cleaners decided to close early – trapping the jacket/trousers/skirt outfit I had planned to take as my 'core wardrobe'. I considered throwing a brick through the window, grabbing my clothes and leaving fifteen quid on the counter, but I was counselled against it by other, more sensible members of my family.

The Coat, though light, is extremely bulky. I wore it in duty free, but kept knocking things off the shelves. The Coat demanded a new sense of spatial awareness; it was made for the great outdoors. I had forgotten that I had come to positively dislike the outdoors and spend most of my time in darkened, overheated interiors. Sweating and gasping, I shrugged The Coat off and got on the plane. The Coat refused to go into the overhead locker. Just as I was about to slam the door on the damn thing, it would insinuate itself out. I trapped it eventually, but only just.

New York was rejoicing in a freak heatwave. The taxi driver who drove me to my hotel wore a T-shirt. People strolled along the sidewalks in Bermuda shorts.

In Miami I sat on the beach in my Wonderbra and knickers, leaving The Coat to sulk in the hotel wardrobe (by that time we weren't speaking).

I'm back in England now and still praying for a cold snap, but I'm beginning to think that The Coat is a useless acquisition, except as a mocking testament to my vanity and folly.

Burglaries

We've been burgled four times in four months. We may as well leave the doors and windows wide open and erect a pink neon sign in the front garden that flashes *House empty. Burglars welcome*. Not that the house needs to be empty for burglars to call on us. The last time they came, my daughter was ill in bed, I was upstairs on the phone, the TV was on in the sitting room and there were three radios playing – all talk stations – but this cacophony of noise still didn't deter them.

Hearing a squeal of tyres, my daughter got out of her sick bed and looked out of her bedroom window to see a battered yellow car being reversed at speed and parked opposite our house. Two ferret-faced boys got out, crossed the road and began to ring our doorbell with some ferocity – rather like the Gestapo used to carry on in old war films. 'I'll have to go,' I said to my sister, 'it sounds like there's a maniac at the door.' My daughter came into my room and told me that she didn't like the look of the two youths. In itself this statement was not unusual – she is notoriously picky when it comes to men. The ringing continued, the letter-box was clattered, the door was booted.

This poor door has been sledgehammered open in previous burglaries and is now permanently out of action. In fact it is no longer a door, it is merely a piece of wood that keeps out the elements, stray dogs, etc. Other people's front doors open; ours does not. Large nails and heavy bolts have been driven into it. The noise stopped and we looked out of the window to see the ferret faces strolling towards the back of the house. I phoned 999 and asked the operator for the police. It could only have been seconds, but it felt like a fortnight before the police answered and I was able to give our address and the fact that two potential burglars were 'climbing over our back garden wall' – because by now we were in the bathroom watching them do just this.

My daughter hurriedly changed out of her teddy-bear pyjamas (not the thing to be wearing when burglars call) into a more assertive, less vulnerable outfit, and went to the window to take the number of the ferret faces' conspicuous yellow car. By now a boy was chiselling away at the French windows at the back of the house. A police patrol car was 'on its way', said the policewoman on the other end of the phone. I handed the phone to my daughter and looked around the upstairs landing for a blunt instrument. Something to give us a few moments should the boys be armed with a knife. But it was a pathetic choice of potential weapons. A bottle of bubble bath? A wooden coat hanger? A loofah on a stick?

Simultaneously I heard the French doors crack open and my daughter whisper, 'Mum, they've put me on hold!' She then shouted down the phone, 'The burglars are in my house!' Adrenaline took over. I was filled with rage – an emotion that doesn't visit me often. I was a lioness defending her cub. There was no way I was going to let the ferret faces upstairs to frighten my daughter, and I was also not going to cower upstairs while they plundered the few possessions we had left from the previous burglaries. I told my daughter to lock herself in her bedroom and crept downstairs.

Ferret face One was in the last room I searched. To say he was gobsmacked when he saw me would be an understatement. His ferrety jaw dropped open at the sight of me, the harridan whose chosen weapon was a book – *Tolstoy* by A. N. Wilson. I didn't need to bludgeon the boy with biography, however – he turned and ran out of the house, slipped in a pile of slimy leaves I had sluttishly left on the garden path, recovered himself and leapt over the wall. Ferret face Two had already preceded him. I shouted, in a voice I didn't know I had, well, perhaps I won't tell you what I shouted, this being a family magazine, but a lot of words in the sentence began with letters to be found in the early part of the alphabet.

I ran round to the front of the house to see the boys trying desperately to start their car. Eventually, in a cloud of exhaust fumes, they managed it and sped up the road with me futilely following on foot. As they turned at the top of the road, a police patrol car passed them. Within forty-five seconds there were three police vehicles outside our house; within another minute there were nine. As I said regretfully to the charming policeman who took down the ferret faces' description, 'I should have waited one more minute.' I've said it to myself many times since then.

Their number plates were false, their fingerprints were blurred. They haven't been caught.

Beige in Cromer

I'm in another hotel, trying to write another film script. The film is set in Barcelona, so where did I choose to go when the producer of the film offered to pay my expenses? Cromer, that's where. Not Cromer USA, or Cromer just outside Barcelona, but Cromer Norfolk. It must be something to do with turning fifty next year because, it has to be said, the visitors to Cromer are not young and hip. I was gloomily looking into a draper's shop window this morning and saw a notice, *Latest Fashion*, £7.99, pinned on to the hem of a hideous sludge-green polyester pleated skirt that was covered in a maple leaf print. I laughed out loud (I've only been here a day and a half but I've already attracted a few curious glances). I may not look as though I'm at the cutting edge of fashion, but I know my *Vogue* and I can't recall seeing a breathily written article urging us readers into polyester pleats.

I left a packet of cigarettes on a shop counter later on and as I was leaving the shop I heard the girl on the till say, 'Whose are these?' A woman customer said, 'They're the woman in black's.' After I'd thanked them both and blamed my poor memory on the menopause and generally made a fool of myself, I walked along the sea front repeating to myself the romantic phrase, The Woman in Black. On the way I passed people only ten years older than me who seemed to be wearing a type of informal uniform: a beige car coat and checked pleated skirt for the women and beige car coat and beige trousers for the men. Both sexes seemed to be wearing the same beige crêpe-soled shoes. The thing I want to know is, will it happen to me? On my sixtieth birthday will I also develop this passion for beige? And what about the permed hair that so many beige-clad older women go in for? Is it compulsory? Does a notice arrive with the pension book?

You are hereby ordered to attend Madame Yvonne's Salon at 1300 hours, where you will be given the regulation perm. Please note that the beige uniform must be worn.

If I was the Great Dictator of the World I would ban beige – it is the colour of compromise and timidity, but I have to admit fear: when we're sixty will my black-clad generation be despised by the generation below us? Will they sneer at our black leather jackets? Will black be the new beige?

There is only one tramp in Cromer. Under the dirt, he is young and handsome. Like most tramps, he is burdened down with bags of rubbish and mysterious bundles. He is quiet and wears black clothes. He has no obvious signs of mental illness. I tried to imagine what brought him to this present state. Was he a writer who came to Cromer to write a film, failed, and is fated to roam the sea front for ever more? Will I be joining him in two weeks?

When I was a child the countryside swarmed with tramps. You could hardly walk down a country lane without bumping into one and, on the whole, they were treated courteously by most people. They were given cups of tea and sandwiches at certain houses on their route, and their advice was sought on the weather and the countryside. I certainly envied them their freedom to roam about and please themselves, especially if I met one dozing by the roadside as I was dragging myself to school.

Cromer is a small place and it seems that every time I turn a corner I come face to face with the handsome tramp. A few hours ago we even shared a bench. We sat together in silence staring at the sunshine on the sea. I am determined not to get to know him. The only relationship I want in Cromer is with my film. I wish my loved one was here, though. I am occupying the honeymoon suite at the Penton-ville Hotel complete with Jacuzzi, brass bed and panoramic sea views.

The sun has gone now and there's a cold wind coming off the sea. I could do with a warm beige car coat.

Pulp Fiction

I've resisted as long as I can, but I've finally cracked. I've got to write about *Pulp Fiction*. I shan't bang on in detail about it (suffice it to say that it is the best film I have ever seen), but I want to try to convey to you the extraordinary effect that the film has had on the people I know. They can't stop talking about it. They quote chunks of the dialogue. They repeat the jokes. They get up and illustrate the dance steps. They discuss their favourite scenes and listen with careful attention while other people discuss theirs, and God knows how many hours have gone by and deadlines missed while I've stuck my own oar in.

The film is about people who make a living from violence; they are contract killers, boxers, soldiers and armed robbers. These people buy and use hard drugs as casually as you or I might buy or use tea bags. Their language is frequently obscene. It is not a film for the kiddiewinkies or your mother (although I've just realized I spent most of last Saturday at a lovely family wedding urging my mother to go and see it).

There was a time earlier this year when my eldest son

was the only member of our branch of the family not to have seen *Pulp Fiction*. He cut a sad, isolated figure, unable to join in PF conversations and remaining straight-faced when the rest of us were cackling at a PF joke. Eventually, although he's now a man of thirty (and starting to notice how ludicrously young doctors are these days), I ordered him to go to the cinema, just like I used to order him to wear a vest when he was a little boy and the weather changed.

It was the making of him. The next day we gathered him back into the bosom of the family and listened joyfully as he brought his own particular intelligence to analysing the film. *Pulp Fiction* has at last given the English an alternative to talking about the weather as a conversational icebreaker. In fact, it often becomes the conversation.

I've been to meetings to discuss my own screenplays and spent most of the time discussing the genius of *Pulp Fiction*'s writer/director, Quentin Tarantino (who is also a mere child). So instead of convincing the producers of my own abilities, I've put myself in the shade. So deep in the shade that nothing is likely to grow. I must stop doing it – it's professional suicide.

I do have an obsessional personality. I wasn't content to simply love Elvis – I wrote to him and asked him to marry me when I reached the legal age of sixteen. (And I also suffer from self-delusion. I expected him to reply and say he was thinking about it.) My next serious obsession was with the writer Dostoevsky. At one time I was never without one of his books on my teenage person. Had he been alive at the height of my passion, I would have trekked to Leningrad and stood in the snow and begged him for a clipping from his beard.

John Travolta stars in *Pulp Fiction* and my daughters have fallen for him all over again. This is a bit worrying because he plays a lank-haired, pasty-faced, overweight piece of lowlife. He would be the son-in-law from hell.

For those of you who haven't seen *Pulp Fiction*, I urge you to see it; despite its violent subject matter, it is a highly moral film. The dialogue is witty and clever and you care passionately about the characters as they progress through the story. I've seen it three times. I've bought the published screenplay, a cassette of the music and the video. If John Travolta dolls went on sale tomorrow, I'd buy one. What am I talking about? I'd buy three.

A sad consequence of my current obsession is the cooling relationship between me and the few people I know who dislike the film. The theatre critic Ken Tynan wrote: 'I couldn't love anybody who doesn't love *Look Back in Anger*.' Other people have said the same of the film *Casablanca*, which is now every film critic's choice.

If only I could develop an obsessive passion for ironing or early rising or completing deadlines. How much easier my life, and the life of the editor of Sainsbury's *The Magazine*, would be. Go and see it, please.

I Have to Have Liver

I'm not a well woman. I've got bronchitis. I took to my bed for a few days (oh, all right, four glorious days of sleep, meals on trays, antibiotics, listening to the radio, watching the clouds and doing nothing). The coughing was a damned nuisance to me and everybody else in the house, and at times I felt very poorly and was damp-eyed with horrible self-pity. But I have to admit that I enjoyed myself enormously.

My husband cooked me the type of meal that used to be served up to Edwardian invalids: huge quantities of comfort food, gravy and custard. He even lined the tray with a clean tea towel. I ate every last crumb. I was like a wolf woman. In fact, one day at 3 a.m. I woke in a bronchitic sweat to find my husband in an exhausted sleep beside me (it's not easy cooking for Wolf Woman), and I had to have liver – nothing else would do.

I staggered downstairs and rummaged through the never-to-be-eaten food at the bottom of the freezer. Eventually I found it – a packet of lambs' liver. It was encrusted in icicles, and must have been there since Mario Lanza topped the hit parade. I averted my eyes from the use-by date and slung the icy bag into the microwave. While it spat and melted I hacked at an onion and some potatoes. It was the SAS Brutalist School of Cookery.

When the liver was reasonably defrosted, I threw it into a roasting tin and chucked it in the oven. Then I paced up and down and waited for it to cook. Half an hour later, I wiped my wolf chops of liver and onions and mashed potato and went back to bed. My husband was baffled by the evidence of my early morning saturnalia. 'Why liver?' he asked. 'It needed using up,' I said feebly, between coughs.

An illness of some kind had been predicted for me by friends and family ever since I announced that I was going to Australia for seven days and would be visiting three cities: Melbourne, Sydney and Adelaide. Max Stafford-Clark, the theatre director, and I had business out there, setting up an Australian tour of *The Queen and I*. Because of my addiction, I couldn't face twenty-three hours without a fag, so I petitioned to fly with Malaysia Airlines, which still allows a few social deviants to sit at the back of the plane and puff on the deadly weed.

Max sat in the middle of the plane, guarding his clean lungs, but we met up in Kuala Lumpur at Dunkin' Donuts, where we tried to decide whether the fiery red ball in the sky was the sun going down or the sun coming up. Incidentally, the duty free shopping mall at Kuala Lumpur stretches as far as the eye can see, but after walking its length and breadth with a fistful of credit cards, I emerged with nothing – not a thing. I should have taken this as a symptom of serious illness and demanded to see a doctor. Shopping isn't really my middle name – it's Lilian – but it's an activity I'm very fond of, though just lately the only things I seem to buy are nailbrushes and cushions.

Australia was wonderful – too wonderful as it turned out. Max and I were looking for a suitably squalid location in which to exile the Queen (my fictional Queen). Most normal people want to see the sights, areas of outstanding beauty, etc. Not us. 'We want to see a poor, run-down area,' said Max to the cab driver in Melbourne. God knows the man did his best, but after driving through what looked to us like endless affluent suburbs, he knew he'd failed us. It was the same story in Sydney and Adelaide.

Of course, there was comparative poverty, but nothing like Britain's grey, cold council estates. However, I did discover a new scene for the Australian version of the play in a pub in Sydney. We saw a list of coming attractions. 'Barmaid's Jelly Wrestling. Monday Night. Five Dollars'. Then, in brackets, 'First Two Rows Free'. A jelly-wrestling scene involving a younger member of the Royal Family would give the play a gritty Australian authenticity, we decided, and jelly was so redolent of aristocratic nursery teas. I can hear nanny now: 'Diana, eat your bread and butter first and then you can wrestle in your jelly.'

I've just realized that it's at least two hours since I had a good cough. This is a serious blow. It means I'm getting better. I may have to cook tonight.

Nudity

I used to be quite a sporty girl. At one time I was never happier than when I was hurdling or long-jumping or bashing at a shuttlecock. Naturally, this all took place at school. The only strenuous exercise I've taken since I left South Wigston High School For Girls, at the age of fifteen, has taken place in the labour ward of a maternity hospital: I've pushed hard for England four times.

But however much I enjoyed games lessons, they were always haunted by the dreaded spectre of the compulsory showers at the end. Thirty girls would be crowded into an echoing, white, tiled room and ordered to strip. We would then be lined up and ordered to walk through the shower room, where alternating jets of hot and cold water seared down on our poor self-conscious English bodies. The only girl in our class who seemed to enjoy compulsory showers, indeed flaunted herself in them, had a very exotic foreign name. I won't reveal it here because she knows things about me (youthful misdemeanours, quite trivial back-of-the-bike sheds stuff, but even so). Quite often I would try to rush through the shower wearing my Aertex top and gym knickers, hoping that the other girls and the steam would hide me; sometimes I got away with it, but mostly I was caught by Mrs Scruton, the games mistress, and ordered to go through again, naked.

I was ludicrously modest in those days. Art galleries were fraught with potential embarrassment, and even the bare-breasted statues in the Town Hall square caused me to blush and look down at my sensible school shoes. I sometimes forged notes:

Dear Mrs Scruton,
   Susan has been up all night with her stomach. Please do not let her take a shower as this could make her worse.
   Yours sincerely, etc.

Mrs Scruton could spot a forged note at 250 paces. She would raise a bushy eyebrow and wordlessly hand back the note, then stand by my peg as I squirmed out of my clothes. When communal changing rooms in shops came in, I stopped buying clothes. Wearing a swimsuit on the beach was an act of great courage – even then I wouldn't really move about, I'd sit rigidly on my towel behind a newspaper. If my children needed help with their sandcastles, I'd shout advice at them, like a football manager, from the sidelines.

The few people to see me naked did so in Stygian darkness. When miniskirts came in, I turned the hems of my existing skirts up by a daring two inches. (I think this is probably the last time I held a needle in my hand.) All this, dear reader, because I thought I was fat. Convinced that I was a blubbering tub of lard whose wobbling flesh must be kept from public gaze.

I was looking at old photographs recently and realized

that, apart from a year when I inexplicably blew up to twelve stone, I have never been fat. The fat git I saw scowling back from the mirror was not me. I was filled with regret. All those years hiding in maxi-skirts and big jumpers when I could have been running about in bikinis, playing volleyball on the beach. Well, perhaps not volleyball, but I could at least have stuck a flag in the odd sandcastle.

I am now in my fiftieth year and feel compelled to make the most of every opportunity, so when I went to Skyros to teach writing I didn't spend my time skulking on the nearest beach in a one-piece bathing suit. I put my shoulders back, stiffened my resolve (I teach my writers never to use clichés) and trekked to 'Bare-Arsed Beach' where I took all my clothes off, in public, in daylight, in front of people I knew. It was a wonderfully liberating experience. People did not run from the beach covering their eyes screaming, 'For God's sake, cover yourself woman'. No thunderbolt came from the sky. Me and my fellow nudists lay and talked about gardening, builders, the nature of existence and the price of teabags. Then, wearing only a baseball cap and a pair of watersports sandals, I paddled a surfboard along the water's edge. Mrs Scruton would have been proud of me.

Heatwave

Tuesday My husband has just come back from the all-night garage with bags full of lemonade and other nice things to add to vodka. Leicester's medical officer has warned we citizens of the town that we must drink at least three litres of liquid a day (daytime temperatures hit 92°F). We are following his advice assiduously.

Nobody is that keen to cook. The Aga is like a fiery monster in the kitchen, but we can't switch it off. Two and a half years ago, in deep winter, we smugly decided to be Aga purists – no running to supplementary gas rings for us, we declared. We now live with the results of our puritanism.

We have been burgled again recently – five times in six months, so the house is now like a top-security wing. I could offer lodging to the train robbers and, providing they didn't have a set of keys, they'd never get out of the house. So, with every window locked and every door double locked and reinforced, nothing gets into our house, including fresh air.

Meanwhile, the Aga is throwing out hot air like a small volcano. I look back, damp-eyed, to the days when I left the house with the windows wide open, the door unlocked, and Radio 4 left on loudly in the kitchen. I stupidly believed that potential burglars would arrive on the doorstep, hear Sue Lawley asking her current castaway what luxury they would take to the island, then tiptoe away with an empty swag bag.

The above sentence, of course, is grammatically ambiguous. It could be read that Sue Lawley tiptoed away with a swag bag. I am not suggesting for a moment that Sue Lawley is a burglar; the very idea is unthinkable. She earns a good salary and her face is too well known. Though it is possible she could get away with it if she wore one of her own silk stockings over her face.

But anyway, the thought of Sue Lawley leaving Broadcasting House, driving to a quiet suburb, changing into an Armani burglary outfit to do a little genteel breaking and entering is quite absurd. Though, of course, you never really know about people.

Wednesday It is 9.30 in the morning and God only knows what the temperature is. Remember those photographs that used to appear on the front pages of the tabloid press of people frying eggs on the bonnets of their cars? The headline above would say, 'Phew, what a scorcher!' I swear it is that hot today. Delia Smith could cook a full English breakfast on my forehead, including fried bread.

I hope you celebrated Flea Week recently. Our cat Max certainly did. He brought vast amounts of them into the house, where they made themselves at home. Remember that song, 'C'mon over to my house, hey hey, we're having a party'? Well, they did come over to my house. When people ask me what the red swollen lumps are on my legs,

I mumble, 'mosquito bites' and reach for the flea spray. It's an uphill battle because the fleas adore the hothouse temperature at our place. It turns them on: when they are not jumping out and biting my legs, they are jumping on to each other. My sofas and chairs and carpets are now flea maternity wards. You can practically hear the champagne corks popping.

Midday, 93 °F All around me people are complaining about the heat. But it's our own fault if we can't cope. We have to change our habits, especially our clothes. A man has just walked past my window wearing a pinstriped business suit, waistcoat, shirt, tie and heavy brogue shoes. Would that man stroll along the promenade at Torremolinos in the same inappropriate outfit? Of course not. He'd be in an Englishman's holiday uniform – too-short running shorts, off-white vest, black socks, sandals and a plastic-trimmed captain's hat. He'd still look ludicrous, but at least he'd be dressed to suit the weather.

I felt a strong temptation to throw open the window and shout, 'Take your clothes off', but I didn't. By the time I'd have found the key and unlocked the window, he'd have gone, and anyway my words could have been misinterpreted. He could have thought I was a mad, middle-aged woman who'd been affected by the heat. Whereas the truth is that I am a mad, middle-aged woman who has been affected by the burglars, the Aga, the fleas, but not the heat.

Hosepipe Ban

I was walking through the grounds of Crystal Palace many years ago when I saw a notice board which was placed in the middle of a flower bed. Written on it, in large black letters, was the following notice: 'Do not throw stones at this notice board.' Puzzling. Surreal even. If the notice board hadn't been there in the first place, how could anybody throw stones at it? What was its purpose except as an example of officialdom gone mad?

Officialdom has been flexing its bossy muscles lately. I am a customer of Severn Trent Water and, at the time of writing, I am forbidden to use my hosepipe. This has deprived me of one of my greatest pleasures. I truly love my garden. I know every plant, every shrub, every tree. It hurts me to see them thirsty and wilting. I've given up on the lawn: it turned into a sullen delinquent years ago and is now totally beyond my control – if it's not careful, I'll turf it out and lay slabs.

I used to love directing a fine spray towards the parched plants and seeing them spring back to life. Watering also did me good. It calmed me down and took my mind off growing old, meeting deadlines and other worries. It was my own particular type of hydrotherapy. Now, since little rain has fallen, I am reduced to lugging heavy watering cans around, which is bad for both my back and my temper. The worst is that Severn Trent Water has engaged helicopters and small planes to fly over its area and report anybody infringing the hosepipe ban.

Can you imagine the ludicrous conversations that must frequently take place between the pilot and Severn Trent HQ?

PILOT: Hose spy plane to HQ. I have a positive sighting. Repeat, I have a positive sighting. Over.

HQ: Details, hose spy plane. Over.

PILOT: 17 Acacia Avenue. Man with bald head wearing spectacles, plaid shirt and army-surplus-type shorts directing hosepipe towards group of sunflowers approximately seven feet tall. Over.

HQ (excitedly): Seven feet tall! He'll be easy to identify then, won't he? Old baldy? Over.

PILOT: No. The sunflowers are seven feet tall. He's turned the hose towards some containers of geraniums now. Want me to take photographs? Over.

HQ: Affirmative. What's he doing now? Over.

PILOT: He's shaking his fist at the sky. Over.

HQ: The computer tells us that he's Arthur Wainwright, a butcher aged fifty-seven. Good work, hose spy plane. We're sending Hose Ban enforcement officers to Acacia Avenue now. Over.

PILOT: What'll happen to him, HQ? Over.

HQ: He'll get fifty lashes with the nozzle end of a hosepipe on his bare buttocks in a public place – usually the car park of a garden centre, a £1,000 fine and confiscation of his hosepipe and outside water tap. Over.

There are areas of the country where milkmen are being encouraged by the authorities to report any suspicious dawn-light activity. The scheme is called Milkwatch. I now look at my milkman in quite a different way and my notes to him have taken on a defensive, slightly paranoic tone.

> *Dear Milkman,*
>
> *I shall only want one pint a day until further notice. This is not because I have murdered my husband – he is alive and well, but he will be away for about a week, in Amsterdam. He assures me that he will not be smuggling diamonds either in or out of the country. Would you please leave me a pint of cream on Saturday, as we are having a small celebration (not to welcome a friend out of jail). Also, next Wednesday I shall need a dozen eggs.*
> *Sue*

Will he reply like this in future?

> *Dear Sue,*
>
> *I'm sorry, but I am not able to supply you with a dozen eggs on Wednesday. John Selwyn Gummer, the cabinet minister, is visiting your locality and, knowing your views on him, I fear you might be tempted to use the aforementioned eggs as projectiles, thus causing a security incident.*
> *Milkman*
> *PS Your cat was meowing on the doorstep at 5.30 this morning. If I find it there again, I will report you to the RSPCA.*

I don't know about you, but in future, after rinsing out my empty milk bottles, I will polish them thoroughly – to remove all fingerprints.

Travelling Through the Snow

Do you miss proper, deep, crunchy snow? The type that immobilizes cars and keeps people at home from work, and children from school? Yes, so do I. A heavy snowfall gives us all a breathing space, and, of course, it looks so beautiful. It softens outlines and gives off a wonderful light. At this time of year I watch the weather forecast and actually listen to what Michael Fish is saying instead of mocking his ties. I want to hear him say that the whole of Great Britain is going to be covered in snow for, well, let's say a month, to include the Christmas holiday. I know this is selfish, and that if I was the driver of a snow plough or a pensioner with unsteady legs, I'd no doubt shake my fists at the clouds overhead; but as I'm not either of these people, bear with me in my fantasy. What I really like is for transport to grind to a halt and a state of emergency to be declared. We don't like to admit it, but we British relish a state of emergency, we lead the world in stoicism, we are secretly made happy when we are forced to queue up for some vital resource. It gives us something to talk about other than *Coronation Street* or the royal family's latest indiscretion.

One of my granddaughters was born during Leicester's last heavy snowfall. She was in a maternity hospital a mile and a half from my house. The roads were blocked with snow. A sensible person would have waited until the next day, when the roads had been tamed by the snow plough and the gritting lorry, but a primitive urge to see and hold this new member of our family took hold of me. I prepared to trek to the maternity hospital as though I were taking part in an Antarctic expedition. I took a flask of tea, food, spare gloves, socks and a torch, and set out.

I know about survival techniques – my husband used to run courses in survival. He would take a group of executives to a remote and inhospitable place, force them to eat worms and charge them rather a lot of money for the privilege.

Anyway, my expedition was not one of the greatest journeys of the world (as I said earlier, it was only a mile and a half), but it was rather marvellous: the sky blazed with stars and as I stumbled along, I felt quite cosmic and brave. I met other snow travellers on the way and we actually spoke to each other and swapped info about our final destinations. One man was making a noble attempt to get to the pub. I watched from a distance as he got to the front door, only to find it closed. His body slumped. I expect Captain Scott slumped in a similar way when told that the Norwegian flag was already flying at the South Pole.

I'm not the fittest woman in the world and I arrived at the maternity hospital in an enfeebled state. The hothouse atmosphere soon had me tearing off my endless layers of clothes. It was a fat, cold woman who entered from the street, but a thin, hot woman who went up in the lift, carrying a bundle of clothes.

The baby had been born with her blue eyes wide open,

and at the age of three hours, they were still open, looking at me. She was worth every icy step. However, I was surprised to see so many other relatives and friends around the bedside. None of them, like me, showed the evidence of a trek in the snow. The women looked well-groomed, glamorous even. I was certainly the only woman there with plastic freezer bags lining (and showing above the tops of) my hefty, fur-lined boots. 'How did you get here?' I gasped. 'In the car,' somebody said. It took the wind out of my sails a bit.

But recently, when the blue-eyed baby – who is now four – couldn't get to sleep, I told her the story of how I had walked through the snow to see her on the day she was born, and she was very pleased. I may have elaborated a little, added a blizzard or two, and I certainly didn't mention that her other visitors had arrived by car.

Incidentally, if you and the children are so desperate to see snow at Christmas that you are thinking of taking a day trip to Lapland to see Santa in his snow-bound grotto, think again. For the past few years, snow has been very thin on the ground there. Thin to the point of nonexistence. Sadly, I have to say that Lapland without snow lacks charm. And it's a long way to go with overexcited children only to end up on a windswept tundra that looks as though it is lit by a 20-watt bulb. I know, I've been there, and I've got the reindeer-horn drinking cups to prove it.

Expelled from the Writers' Club

I lay on my bed fully dressed, with a patch over one eye and sunglasses, and watched my eldest daughter pack my suitcase. I was lying down because I was too tired to stand up, and I was wearing the patch and sunglasses combo because . . . no, it's too boring to go into. It is. It really is.

My daughter's brief was to pack suitable clothes for two weeks on a Greek island in October. The island is called Skyros, which means wind, so this was no easy shorts 'n' T-shirt type of packing. My suitcase is small, the same type that air stewardesses wheel on and off aeroplanes with such economy of movement. I wasn't going on holiday, though; I was going to teach writing to fifteen adults. Not just any old writing: in two weeks they were going to write a poem and their own obituary (sounds morbid, I know, but all the obituaries were funny). They wrote a monologue (as a member of the opposite sex), a radio play, the opening of a film and the first page of their novel.

I always feel a bit of a fraud before I embark on this teaching stint. I haven't got an O level or GCSE to my name, and the only time I ever set foot in a university as a young woman was to enter a twist competition. While we're at it, I may as well confess to failing my 11-plus and also (this is truly humiliating) my cycling proficiency test. I think you'll agree that these non-qualifications are best kept from nervous writing students. I have been working as a professional writer for eighteen years, but I am still expecting a fax message saying:

To: Sue Townsend
From: The Society for the Exposure of Unworthy Writers
You have been found out. You must leave the writing profession immediately. A vacancy has been found at the biscuit factory. You will be packing Bourbon Creams from 7.30 a.m. to 5.30 p.m., six days a week, at a speed determined by the management. An overall and an unflattering hairnet must be worn at all times.
Yours sincerely,
Edna Grubbe
Secretary

I can hear some of you muttering, 'About time too.' Most of the writers I know are waiting for the same kind of calamity to befall them. Writers are driven creatures, beset with anxieties and having the confidence of a retarded lugworm. If somebody at a party tells me my last book or play was rubbish, I don't run weeping from the room, I agree with them. 'Yes!' I laugh happily. 'You've found me out, I'm not a proper writer!' The writers I know all feel the same way. There are two exceptions. Both men. Small men. One has a beard, the other is fat. Both are best-sellers. I'd love to give you their names. My pen is itching to . . . but as I don't want to spend weeks in the High Court or give a barrister £1,000 a day to defend me on a defamation charge, I'll draw back from the brink.

No, I can't let the subject drop. These men think every sentence they write is precious and perfect and wasted on their swinish readers. I read an interview with one of these men recently – the bearded one: 'Writing is a job,' he said. 'I don't lie awake worrying about it.' I threw many curses at the photograph of his horrible, smug face and remembered the statement about writing with which I most closely identify: 'writing is easy, all you have to do is stare at a blank piece of paper until your forehead bleeds'.

So, I arrived on the island with a bundle of insecurities and anxieties, a bag of medication, and a face free of make-up – a rare and sorry sight. I had left my cosmetics bag in the lavatory at Athens airport. Some lucky woman is swanning around with my duty-free Chanel lipstick on her thieving chops.

Within two days, the writers' group bonded. We laughed ourselves stupid, cried occasionally, had our siestas, then danced and made very merry indeed in the evenings. We also worked extremely hard.

It was only towards the end of the second week that I let slip that I was not in any way qualified to teach writing. But by then they didn't care; they had all written something they were proud to read aloud. I admire teachers, but I couldn't bear to teach in Britain. The teaching aids I need are a sunlit, terraced classroom with a sea and mountain view, a taverna-lined main street, cobbled and too narrow for cars. Bougainvillaea, vines heavy with grapes, trees decorated with pomegranates, Greek salads, a fantastical townscape of white cubist houses climbing up a hillside, and a late-night bar serving extravagantly large drinks and playing smoky jazz until 3.30 a.m. I'll have to blag it out with the writing. I couldn't possibly get up at 7.30 a.m. to pack the Bourbon Creams, and I'd look hideous in that hairnet.

To Do List

1 p.m. **I've just** come back from visiting my dentist after a gap (perhaps the word should be cavity) of six years. I kept meaning to ring for an appointment but somehow never got round to it. It has been on my List of Important Things To Do for . . . well, six years.

I have seen my dentist in the intervening years but it wasn't in his surgery; it was in the bar of the Haymarket Theatre. He kindly bought me a drink and I promised to ring him, but unfortunately I was on strong painkillers (for toothache) at the time. I think they must have affected my memory because it quite slipped my mind to ring him for an appointment. My dentist is a kind man, patients travel from abroad to see him. He is a hero to my children. His work is painless. He cares about each tooth in your head, so I can't explain the six-year gap.

'I will treat you as if you are two-and-a-half years old,' he once said to me reassuringly. I think he is the only man I've ever known to recognize my true age.

My List of Important Things To Do is (not in order of importance):

1 Make and sign a will
2 Throw sequined sweaters out of the wardrobe
3 Have sewerage pipes x-rayed
4 Ring dentist
5 Walk two miles a day
6 Finish 50,000-word novel
7 Transfer conifer from tub to permanent place in garden
8 Reply to 1994 letters
9 Throw away all underwear ruined in wash
10 Reply to 1995 letters

Perhaps I could take this opportunity to apologize to friends and strangers who may have written to me in 1994 and 1995. I intend to reply to your letters one day. It's just that I let things slip in 1995 and now, in 1996, I have this towering, slithering mountain of correspondence that I shall need oxygen to conquer.

4.30 p.m. I've decided to tackle the list. I've just been upstairs and taken the sequined sweaters out of the wardrobe and then trawled through cupboards and drawers for underwear casualties. I don't know about you, but whenever I buy new underwear I swear to myself that I'll handwash it in special lotion, that I'll pat it dry with absorbent paper and I'll iron it on a special low setting. So why is it that I've just rounded up a pile of sad, grey garments that are about as alluring as John Major's upper lip? I could blame my husband – who is currently out of the country selling canoes to Scandinavians – but that wouldn't be fair.

I'm going shopping now, so there isn't time for the two-mile walk, but who knows? When I come back, perhaps

I'll take a stroll around the neighbourhood and check out the security lights on the neighbours' houses.

As for x-raying the sewerage pipes, well, quite honestly I can't face it. I keep remembering the emergency plumber's face when he broke the news to us that the pipe (which runs under the kitchen floor, for some inexplicable reason) seemed to have 'restricted flow'. His expression was grave – how an actor playing a TV doctor looks when he or she is informing an actor patient that they've got a fortnight to live. No. I'll face the pipes x-ray when I feel stronger in body and in mind. There's only so much a woman can do, especially a heavily burgled woman such as myself.

So, that leaves the pipes, the will and the novel. I don't know if you have written your will. It does concentrate the mind wonderfully. You sit there with your solicitor and advisers chatting merrily about their life after your death.

Any eccentric thoughts you may have about imposing conditions on the beneficiaries ('I leave each of my children x pounds each, providing they never marry, go to church twice on Sunday and breed pigs') are quickly dismissed, and the solicitor gently guides you into more prosaic language.

2.20 a.m. Today, I've been shopping and bought enough food for a siege. I've given a telephone interview to a journalist in Australia and I've written 1,000 words of the novel, but I can't help asking – what's it all about, Alfie? Is it just for the moment we live?

Perhaps the lists we all make represent the future. But whatever they damn well mean, there must be more to life than ticking off the items, one by one.

Abusive Letters

I'm probably the only person I know who doesn't mind receiving anonymous letters – at least I don't have to reply to the damn things. My first came some years ago; it accused me of funding the IRA, and he/she (but I think *he*) said they would kill me, 'at the theatre, in front of your family and friends'. My children urged me to go to the police with it, but quite honestly I was not shaking in my shoes – there was something about the handwriting and the phrasing that told me the writer of the letter could hardly hold a Biro straight, let alone aim a Kalashnikov rifle accurately.

I have another regular, anonymous correspondent whose envelopes are so covered in mad scribbling and crazed insults that a couple of them have been intercepted by the Post Office and subsequently handed over to the police. This person accuses me of being heavily involved in council and police corruption. Apparently, I have several Leicester City councillors in my power and I spend my nights at the council offices, 'smoking your foul cigarettes, and plotting your next move'. If only one *could* smoke in the council offices. The days of the smoke-filled room are long gone, unfortunately.

Last week's anonymous letter consisted of two pages written in red ink; it accused me of being the spurned lover of the Prince of Wales! She started the letter: 'Just to say, Sue, you are a BITCH!' There were a few more abusive paragraphs, then this: 'I am certain that you are one of Prince Charles's cast-off lovers.' This woman objected to some critical remarks I'd made about Princess Diana.

She went on to write, 'Just try to be a woman for once in your life, just pretend to be a woman and imagine how a woman would feel when she had been badly treated by a man.' She signed the letter, 'A *Daily Mail* reader'.

Here's my reply.

Dear Daily Mail *reader,*

Thank you for your anonymous letter. You are entirely wrong in your supposition that I am the spurned and jealous ex-lover of Prince Charles. I couldn't fancy a man who habitually wears a blazer. Men in blazers remind me of crooked insurance salesmen. I also dislike those slip-on patent slippers Prince Charles wears to evening functions. I like my men to wear chunky shoes.

I realize that, so far, my refutation of your wild premiss is based entirely on what may seem to you to be frivolous, sartorial grounds, but these things are important to me. I once fell instantly out of love with a man because he returned from the barber's with his hair cut too short.

You ask me to imagine what it is like to be badly treated by a man. Excuse me while I larf. I am fifty next year. I went out with my first boy/man when I was fourteen. I don't need to imagine what it is like to be badly treated by a man. I gave up acting at sixteen because a man said I looked 'bloody stupid' on stage. I tried to hide my profile for years because another man chucked me and gave as his reason, 'your nose is too big'. I could go on, but I won't. There are too many instances of similar male cruelties.

Believe me, I have every sympathy with Princess Diana's marital dilemma. There may well have been four people in her marriage, but the fourth person was not me. I have been far too busy with my family and my work to indulge myself in a royal romance, and, anyway, what makes you think Charles would be attracted to me? I'm scared of horses and would be hopeless on the moors, shooting at birds and small animals. Finally, I have never laughed at The Goon Show. I would leave the room instantly if Charles started doing his infamous Goon impressions. I'm a Jack Dee woman.

Have I succeeded in convincing you that Prince Charles and I have not had a torrid affair? I hope so. I also hope that you have not blabbed your mad suspicions to your neighbours and friends, or to the stationer where you buy your horrible red pens.

I must warn you, Daily Mail reader, that, should it come to my attention that you have been publicly linking Charles and myself, I will set several Leicester City councillors (whom I have in my power) on to you. You have been warned.

Yours sincerely,
Sue Townsend
(Marxism Today and Daily Telegraph reader)

Out on the Razz

On Tuesday of this week I had the great pleasure of participating in an event that gave money to the deserving poor. It was nothing to do with the Lottery, though the poor people in this case were playwrights, and they had won £5,000 apiece.

The Pearson Television Playwrights Scheme organizes this annual prizegiving. Their motives, though laudable, are not entirely altruistic. Television needs writers. Without writers it would turn its tube to the corner of the room and die. It's a fact that quite a lot of seemingly intelligent television reviewers do not realize that writers are involved in the production of a drama. Actors are used to fans approaching them in the street and saying, 'I saw you in that thing on TV last night. I don't know how you make those words up on the spur of the moment, but what you said was very clever/very funny/made me cry.'

A few actors accept this badly misguided praise. 'How very kind,' they murmur modestly whilst scribbling their immodest, flamboyant signatures inside the fan's autograph book or whichever crumpled piece of paper is dredged up from the bottom of a handbag. Other, more honest, actors tell the blunt truth: 'I don't make the words up. A writer does.' But this does not usually go down too well. It's a bit like trying to explain to a ten-year-old child that Michael Jackson used to be black or that Dame Edna Everage is actually a man called Barry Humphries who has a taste for high culture and a particular interest in classical literature.

So I am obviously pleased to be a part of a scheme that celebrates and encourages young playwrights. In truth, they are not that young, but these things are relative. I'm used to seeing twelve-year-old policemen flexing their batons. I was in a shop recently when a fraught customer, holding a faulty purse, called for the manager. To my surprise, I saw an eight-year-old girl stroll out of the back room. This child (who should have been at home playing mummies and daddies with Barbie and Ken) proceeded to reel off a whole clause of the Consumer Protection Act as it related to the purse, whose press stud had fallen off some three months earlier. Anyway, I mustn't get sidetracked, though I have to say that, unusually for me, my sympathies this time lay with the shop. The owner of the purse looked to me as though she'd be very heavy on a press stud. She'd obviously violently wrenched her purse open one too many times; and anyway, why wait three months to complain? She said herself that she worked in the town. Why not call in and complain on the first day that the purse failed to fasten? Anyway, I mustn't get sidetracked. But I'll just tell you the outcome of this small human drama. The child/manageress offered the woman a credit note for the cost of the purse (which was very magnanimous of her, I thought). The complainant then cast a cursory eye over the huge range of purses on sale and declared that she didn't like a single one of them and wanted £9.99 cash in hand. At this point, I wanted to join in and remonstrate with the purse woman, but I managed to draw back from the brink, only allowing myself to signal my solidarity with the child/manageress by a system of smiles and eye-rolling. Anyway, as I said earlier, I mustn't get sidetracked.

After the playwrights' cheques had been handed out, there was a small reception: drink was taken, vegetables were dipped, and we posed for photographs. Eventually, people drifted away, leaving only the playwrights, a playwright's dancer girlfriend, a few bottles of wine and myself. A dangerous combination.

Much, much later, our party fell into a black cab, and the last I saw of the playwrights and the dancer was them standing in a Soho street waving happily as my cab sped me to St Pancras station and the train to Leicester.

At 11.30 p.m. I phoned my husband from the train using the words that are so mocked by those who despise mobile phones: 'Hello. I'm on the train.' I had slept past Kettering, Market Harborough and Leicester, and God knows where else, and awoke to find myself in a stationary train on a dark, deserted railway station. My footsteps echoed as I walked out of the station. Nottingham was devoid of humans. Taxi drivers were snoring under their duvets. A man wearing a neck brace let me into a small hotel near the station. 'Cash only,' he said suspiciously. I've rarely seen so much Formica in such a small space, but I slept soundly enough. In the morning I looked out of the bedroom window and saw that the canal, murky and deep, lay below. I thought briefly about throwing myself in but decided that life, even for somebody as stupid as me, has to go on.

Dream House

'**There's a house** with a wood for sale in Quorn,' I said casually. My husband knows that under my mild-mannered, good-humoured persona lies another person: a cross between Pol Pot and Joan Crawford. I never make casual remarks. Accordingly, he got the message and switched on the indicator and we turned towards Quorn.

Quorn is not the headquarters of the meat substitute so beloved of vegetarians, it is a large village full of des reses. The hip'n'thigh flat stomach magnate Rosemary Conley lives there. In fact, the river that makes the village so 'des' runs through her property. I expect it pulls its stomach in as it rushes by.

The house was called One Ash. There was a picture of a bad-tempered, growling Alsatian on the padlocked gate. I can't remember whether I climbed over the gate or limbo'd beneath it. I was in a fever of excitement because I had seen the wood.

Recent photographs of me may suggest that I spent my infancy, childhood and adult life in a subterranean nightclub, but I grew up surrounded by woods. As a small child I climbed the trees and made dens in the scrubby under-growth. I collected conkers and acorns in the autumn, and picked the celandines and primroses in the spring. In the summer I took a bottle of water and a jam sandwich and had a picnic in the dark shade, and in the winter, in the snow (it always snowed when I was a child), I would take great delight in being the first to put my wellington prints on to the snowy woodland floor. I got to know each tree very well, and when most of the wood was cut down to make way for housing, I was heartbroken.

'It's going cheap because it's been vandalized,' I said to my husband as we walked up the long driveway through the wood. 'But it's thirteen acres.' He didn't flinch. He didn't point out that we found it difficult to find the time to tend our present garden, which is the size of a large slice of bread and has only five trees. We couldn't yet see the house, but we saw a paddock in the distance. We passed an overgrown tennis court with a sagging net, and a piece of open ground with a summer house.

Then we turned a corner and walked up a slight incline, and there was the house. Dark and boarded-up, looking like something out of a horror film; I expected to see lightning and hear thunder and the sound of a distant scream. We walked round the back of the house to look at the outbuild-ings and the smashed orangery and greenhouses. A swim-ming pool was full of slime and rubbish, but the garden – even in winter – was lovely. There were ponds and a brick-built pergola, and everywhere trees and the glorious intermingling smells of conifers and rotting leaves. I felt weak with desire. I wanted it. I wanted it before I had seen the front of the house, or been inside it. I could see my grandchildren running through the woods. I could see myself writing in the summer house. I could see my husband replacing every single one of the hundred panes of glass in the orangery. (Strangely enough, he didn't share this particular vision.)

When I saw the front of the house, I thought I would faint with pleasure. There were shutters and a pretty Edwardian wrought-iron balcony, and a lovely front door. A pale man covered in coal dust came out. He was carrying a torch. Did we 'want to see inside the house'?

'Yes,' I wanted to shout, 'of course we want to see inside the house. It is our house. We are going to live here.'

The batteries were going in the pale man's torch, and every window was boarded up from the outside, so we stumbled around in deep blackness. But I did glimpse beauti-ful window frames, ceilings, floors and fireplaces, and vowed that I would live here and make it light and warm and welcoming. We thanked the pale man and he went back to huddle over his coal fire.

I was back the next day with my sister Kate and my two daughters. Kate was enthusiastic, but the girls recoiled in horror. We drove to the estate agents, where a young man told me that the house was about to be sold, for cash.

'Anyway,' said my relieved daughter, looking at my disconsolate face as we drove home. 'You couldn't live in a house called One Ash.'

'What would you call it?' I asked her as I lit yet another cigarette. 'Fag Ash?' she suggested. We all laughed, but my laughter was more hollow than theirs.

Max the Fat Cat

I swore I'd never do this: join the columnists who write about their damned cats.

Our cat has gone mad. He sits in the front hall and cries to be let out. Once outside he runs around to the back of the house and cries to be let back in. As soon as he's inside again he runs to the hall and cries to be let out. Round and round and round. Does he think he's a goldfish?

His name is Max and I think he suffers from a depressive illness of some kind. He looks like he bears the problems of the world on his furry shoulders: as though he is in charge of Middle Eastern peace talks or responsible for the compilation of a British Rail timetable. He wears a permanently miserable expression. He has never looked happy, even as a kitten. Perhaps he was taken away from his mother at too early an age, but he never *played*. If you waggled a ball of wool in front of him, he would gaze at it with a bleak expression, like an actor in an Ingmar Bergman film, and then walk away. He was the most joyless kitten I have ever known. He is now ten. One look at his face and I start to question the point of animal and human existence. Why *are* we here?

He has a serious eating disorder; this is because he is also a pathological liar. People come and go in our house all the time, and Max manages to convince each resident and each visitor that he has been starved of nourishment for a week. He has got the loudest and most irritating cat voice I have ever heard. I'm surprised the council's environmental health people haven't been round before now with their decibel counting machine. Sometimes he is fed as much as six times a day. As a consequence he is grossly fat; I've seen motorists slow down and goggle at him as he waddles along the pavement.

He is also stupid. Our house is chock-a-block with sofas and beds. There is even a cat basket, yet the fool chooses to sleep in the centre of the bottom step of the stairs, exactly where the humans need to walk. Naturally his sleep is constantly being disturbed by stumbling, swearing people. If I'm ever found at the foot of the stairs in a crumpled heap, with a fading pulse, you'll know who to blame – Max. And will he mourn for me? I don't think so. I'm just the schmuck who shells out for his cat food.

Another example of his stupidity: he once fell asleep with his head so close to an open fire that he burnt his whiskers off. Consequently, without these aids to width and distance, he was unable to pass through open doorways or yard-wide gaps in hedges until the whiskers had grown back.

I think he hates me. I sometimes turn my head and catch him looking at me with a contemptuous, judgemental expression on his face. He always looks away quickly, but not before he's left me feeling disturbed, anxious and, for some reason, guilty.

I have a friend who is a fanatical cat lover. (You know the type: they visit you in hospital and enquire after your cat's health.) When this cat lover visits our house, Max goes into Orphan Annie mode. He shivers in the corner and whines pitifully. He even manages to make himself look *thin*. And, of course, he has managed somehow to remove his collar and name tag and to tangle his fur up and play host to millions of fleas.

'Poor Max,' she cries, and she swoops him into her arms and kisses his face before feeding him and grooming him and talking to him as though he were a person.

'All he needs is some love and attention,' says the friend reproachfully as she carries the turncoat upstairs to the guest bedroom, where he will sleep with his traitorous head on her pillow. There is no point in protesting to her that the cat is *acting* in an attempt to discredit me. My friend is convinced that the cat is emotionally and physically deprived. When I complained recently about cat hairs on my clothing, she snapped, 'Then stop wearing black.'

Another thing I've got against Max is how badly he treats his cat friends. In particular a pathetic creature with three legs and a sulky face. Sometimes he beats her up in the garden. At other times he invites her to share his dinner. But I don't think Three Legs and Max are having a sexual relationship. He is sexually confused. When he was an adolescent the vet ventured the opinion that Max was homosexual, but in my opinion Max is asexual. Three Legs will never bear his kittens.

Sadly, Max was run over recently. I phoned home with the news. 'How badly was he hurt?' asked my husband. 'About two hundred pounds' worth,' I said, looking at the vet's bill.

Do they prescribe Prozac for cats?

Mr and Mrs Blue Hair

I know that I've been claiming for some time that I'm fifty years old, but I've been working on the Chinese principle that a person's true age should be calculated from the day (or night) of their conception. But I am now, occidentally speaking, fifty. If forty is a dangerous age, then fifty has got to be, well, far more dangerous.

People *retire* at fifty these days. We've all seen the pension advertisements featuring that smugly smiling blue-haired couple striding across the golf course, or taking tea in the garden, their gleaming dentures about to bite into a home-baked scone.

We sometimes see Mr and Mrs Blue Hair sailing their dinghy on what looks like an estuary in Essex. Curiously, although the sail of the dinghy is full of wind, the couple's hair remains helmet-like – not a single blue hair is ever out of place. I feel sorry for Mr and Mrs Blue Hair. Not only are they condemned to using a full can of hair spray before they go sailing, they are also fated to live lives of full-time leisure. Leisure with a capital L.

Judging from the advertisements, their average day

begins with breakfast in a hotel room. Mrs Blue Hair, elegant in a lace-trimmed negligée, Mr in silk dressing gown. Through the window can be seen the immaculate fairways of the hotel golf course, on which they will soon be tramping with the golfing equipment bought with the pension plan.

Lunchtime sees them sitting in the garden of a country pub (thatched) sipping their horrible alcohol-free drinks. The early afternoon is taken up with the aforementioned dinghy sailing. By tea time they are antiques-hunting in a Cotswold village. One of them, usually Mrs Blue Hair, is holding up a hideous artefact for the approval of the other. By early evening they are back in the hotel, dressing for dinner. Mr Blue Hair is fastening the clasp on Mrs Blue Hair's necklace. Sometimes their hands are touching.

Does Mrs Blue Hair fear that Mr Blue Hair will take his hands from the necklace and place them around her neck and strangle her? Perhaps with the cry, 'I cannot stand the thought of spending another minute of leisure with you!' No, of course not. Because there they are, in the hotel restaurant, clinking their long-stemmed glasses together and congratulating each other on their foresight in arranging such a generous pension plan. Even later we see them dancing decorously together, Mr Blue Hair keeping his distance from his wife, unlike many men of his age who have drunk too much and go in for a bit of pelvic thrusting on the dance floor.

And off to bed we presume. But we never actually *see* them in bed. Sex is a leisure activity Mr and Mrs Blue Hair don't appear to indulge in. Presumably because sex is still free (it would be difficult to privatize), and even impecunious people without pension plans are still able to indulge themselves in this pleasurable leisure-time activity. No expensive equipment is needed, unless your tastes are *very* specialized, and the wearing of clothing is positively discouraged, again unless . . .

We do know that Mr and Mrs Blue Hair had a sexual relationship in the past, because we occasionally see them visiting the grandchildren. Though really the grandchildren are an excuse; what the Blue Hairs are doing is showing off again. What they truly want us to see is their new saloon car, and their swanky matching luggage (the car boot is open), bought and paid for by the pension plan.

What we never see is the Blue Hairs bickering over whose turn it is to empty the stinking pedal-bin. We certainly don't see them arguing over the remote control, or complaining that the grandchildren have lost the tiny key to Mrs Blue Hair's vanity case at some time during their visit.

We are not allowed to think that retirement at fifty is anything less than leisure-filled heaven. In the world inhabited by the Blue Hairs, the best things in life are not free. They are bought in shops. Sometimes I see a wistful expression on Mr Blue Hair's face. I think he misses his workplace and his former colleagues.

And Mrs Blue Hair, she's not a happy woman, she wants her old life back, the one she had before he retired. A little light charity work in the morning. A library book and Oprah Winfrey in the afternoon.

Mrs Blue Hair is tired of golf and hotels and country pubs and dinghies, and dancing to the hotel quintet. She wants to slob out and relax and let her blue hair blow in the wind. And so do I.

Lovely Roundabout

There is a large traffic island near to where I live. I pass it nearly every day and always look on it fondly, because this is no ordinary traffic island. Built out of Westmorland stone, it is covered in trees and shrubs and flowers and rockery plants. In the spring, when the bulbs burst into flower, it looks particularly delightful. In the summer, herbaceous plants wave in the breeze, and when these finally die away there is a display of autumn foliage and berries to delight the eye.

This traffic island is a Leicester landmark. I not only admire it, I am also *proud* of it. This may make me sound like the ultimate nerd, but I don't care. There is anger in my bosom because the council transport division wants to replace it with three sets of traffic lights, 'to increase the traffic flow'. When I first heard about this dastardly plan, the blood traffic flow to my heart almost stopped.

Leicester has traffic lights like centipedes have legs. Visitors rub their eyes in disbelief when faced with the sight of Belgrave Road, which looks like an amber, red and green hell. These lights stretch to the horizon and beyond, possibly to infinity. Recently we Leicester citizens have seen the proliferation of painted road markings. Every main road seems to have been painted with diagonal lines, boxes or shark's-teeth patterns, and bigger and bossier signs. They'll be painting 'Stop smoking!' or 'Have you brushed your teeth?' on the damned roads next.

I had better admit right now that I am not a driver, but I have owned a car. It was a cabriolet, grey and sleek, and when I saw it in the window of the car showroom I went in and bought it. (I'd only nipped out for a loaf of bread.) I imagined myself behind the wheel, wearing a headscarf and pigskin driving gloves, driving skilfully down a dangerous mountain pass, somewhere abroad, on my way to the coast. I was chatting and making jokes in fluent French to my companion. (Remember, this was only in my imagination; in real life my French is *très mal*. I once ordered a meal for my children from a French menu and was presented with a huge basket full of raw vegetables that had only recently been torn from the ground.)

I got myself a provisional licence and asked my husband to sit next to me while I drove the sleek, grey cabriolet around the Leicestershire countryside. When I drove along the grass verge he would gently suggest that I might find it more comfortable to drive on the road. When I exceeded the speed limit (by 30 mph) he hinted that it might be a good idea to ease my foot off the accelerator. Emboldened by my jaunts in the countryside, I decided to take a crash course, at the end of which I would take my driving test.

I was recommended to go to a certain driving instructor. Let's call him 'M'. He had a very good reputation and was responsible for many first-time passes. Unfortunately, the week of my crash course was also M's disaster week. Everything that could go wrong with a man's life went wrong in that week. I spent the week driving M from the site of one domestic and business disaster to the next.

It has to be said that I was an unruly pupil. I resented stopping at traffic lights and seemed congenitally unable to keep to the speed limit. Also, I hated driving *behind* anything. Poor M, who was famous for his cool nerves, began to bite his nails. By the seventh day he was twitching somewhat. On day eight I took my test.

Mr Smith was my examiner. After eleven attempts to do a three-point turn I offered to let him leave the car, but he declined. M watched from the first floor of the examiner's headquarters as I stalled the car across two lanes of the dual carriageway. For the first time in a week he was smiling.

I have never driven a car since. My children were thrilled to get their hands on the sleek, grey cabriolet but, after a few weeks of nightmares in which I saw them come to messy ends in the sleek one, I put it up for sale. 'One careful lady driver. 1,000 miles on the clock.' Naturally, nobody believed it and the car sold for far less than I paid for it. So much less that I sometimes wake up in the middle of the night and remember *exactly* how much less.

On Sunday, the 'Save Our Roundabout Campaign' held a protest picnic on the island. I meant to join them but completely forgot. But I want them to know that I'm behind them; so is my family. My ex-brother-in-law has said he will 'do a Newbury' and tie himself to the tree that stands in the middle if the bulldozers dare approach. There is so little that is beautiful in our cities in 1996, so little to gladden the eye. So I beseech Leicester City Council to spare our lovely traffic island. I'm not above threats, either. Destroy that island and I may take up driving again.

In Melbourne

I was in Australia when Isabelle was born. My normal procedure for visiting a newborn grandchild is to storm the maternity hospital, whatever the hour, push through the doors marked 'Private' and grab the child to my bosom and welcome it to the family. I'm normally quite polite when it comes to the social conventions, but when the family are involved I lose all constraint. I think I must have Mafia blood in me. I haven't inherited the drug-dealing and contract-killing gene, but I think I may have inherited the 'family-first' gene. I've probably passed it on to my sons. Last year my youngest daughter's potential boyfriends had to pass a series of scrupulous tests of character and have their past histories examined. The poor girl was like a princess in a fairy tale. Suitor after suitor was rejected. She would often return from a night out with a sad story about the Townsend brothers escorting yet another hapless youth away from her side on the dance floor. His crime was sometimes very trivial (he was known to habitually wear white socks), or more serious (being a serial womanizer with several children scattered around the East Midlands).

My sons assured me that they were saving their sister a lot of heartbreak, and perhaps they were right. She now has a very nice boyfriend who has the full approval of all the family. My eyes lit up when I heard that he was a plumber. I have spent a fortune on the mad plumbing in our house over the years, so it will be marvellous to have a plumber on tap. I am encouraging the girl to have a long-term romance.

Isabelle is two-and-a-half weeks old now, and I haven't seen her or held her yet. She looks beautiful in the photograph my husband brought out to me. I can't stop showing this photograph to strangers. So far I have shown it to a woman I spoke to in a toilet in Sydney, a Greek taxi driver, an assistant in a dress shop in Melbourne, and anybody else who will slow down long enough to look. I'm already grateful to Isabelle because she gave her mother so little pain. Four gentle contractions and she was born, which surprised everyone present – especially the mother, who asked, 'Is that my baby?' So take heart, pregnant women everywhere – it could happen to you.

I am in Melbourne at the moment publicizing the opening of *The Queen and I*, my play about the Queen and the royal family being exiled to an outer suburb of Sydney. I did a live radio interview last week, and a woman called Sylvia rang in and said I should be thrown off the top of the radio station building (twenty-two storeys). She then calmed down somewhat and said I should be hanged by my neck from the flagpole. But ardent monarchists such as Sylvia are quite thin on the ground here in Australia. In fact, Britain has very little influence on the everyday life of Australians. English fashion is the exception, but one wonders why: Australian designers use wonderful fabrics and cutting techniques, and make their clothes for all ages and sizes of women – not just for teenage stick insects.

It is winter here and Australians are walking around in an incredible variety of clothes. Somebody wearing a T-shirt, shorts and flip-flops can be followed down the street by a person dressed in big boots, moleskin trousers, a sweater and a greatcoat. The only dress rule I have seen on the window of restaurants and bars states: 'Shoes must be worn'.

I was having breakfast in a hotel this morning when I looked up and saw my name in big letters outside the theatre opposite. I almost choked on my boiled egg. To succeed in persuading a thousand people a night to leave their homes and go to a theatre to watch a play seems an impossible thing to do. At this moment I am beset by fear and anxiety. This makes me clumsy. The director, Max Stafford-Clark, purses his lips in the rehearsal room as a pile of my rewritten pages slithers to the floor. I know I am the writer from hell and I wouldn't work with me again for a million pounds.

I think the editor of this magazine must be cursing the day he invited me to be a contributor. 'Where's Townsend's copy?' I can hear him shouting (though he is the mildest, most even-tempered of men). The fact that I am 12,000 miles away is no excuse for the fact that this article is now four days late. Fax machines have made such excuses redundant. So, what can I blame? Jet lag? No, I'm over that now. Laziness? No – if only I had the *time* to be lazy. No, it's the fear of putting words down on paper. I think I am suffering from wordaphobia. I may have to consult a doctor and ask him or her to send a sick note to the editor.

Plane Trauma

The preview audiences for *The Queen and I* (the Australian version) laughed their socks off. But the first-night audience only laughed one sock off and the newspaper critics kept both socks resolutely on; to say that they loathed the play would be a gross understatement. I sat up in bed in my hotel room in Melbourne and read the reviews, then sank back on to the pillows while words such as 'puerile', 'unfunny' and 'sitcom' danced in front of my eyes. I think at some stage I might have pulled the blankets over my head and whimpered. I know that when I emerged into the daylight I looked longingly towards the minibar, where instant oblivion – in the form of strong alcohol – resided, but as it was only 8.30 in the morning I made myself a cup of tea instead. I then did my packing and left for the airport.

I had delayed my return to England by one day because I wanted a smoking flight, but when I checked in, a clean-cut youth informed me that the flight was now non-smoking. I nearly burst into tears (if there are any children reading this, never put a cigarette between your lips. *Never.* You will have a permanent cough, you will stink, and you will humiliate yourself in front of youths at airport check-in desks). The entire airport is non-smoking, so I stood outside in the company of other addicts and smoked many cigarettes until the 'now boarding' sign flashed. Each fag tasted disgusting, but an addict is addicted, so they *had* to be smoked.

'What about willpower?' I hear you mutter. 'What about it?' I reply. I have no willpower. The part of my brain that controls willpower has been invaded by the nicotine-craving gang, and they take no prisoners.

The plane took off normally enough, but as we began to climb I noticed some discomfort in my ears. My fellow passengers began shaking their heads and poking their ears with their fingers. Babies began to scream. By the time the captain announced that the plane had reached its cruising height of 35,000 feet I thought my head was going to burst. Then the oxygen masks came down. The only time I had seen that happen before was on aeroplane-disaster movies. Being English, I kept my head, though I did turn to the man in the grey suit next to me and smile. A novelist would have called it a wry smile. Mr Grey Suit raised his eyebrows and took the oxygen mask dangling in front of him and placed the rubber mouthpiece over his mouth. I did the same. No oxygen came out. The cabin crew were nowhere to be seen, and the captain was now worryingly silent. Meanwhile, the pressure inside my head was becoming intolerable. The cause could have been delayed shock brought on by the terrible reviews, but I've had bad reviews before without my head bursting.

Diagonally opposite me sat a man who could have been the fattest man in Australia on his way to represent his country in an international fat man competition. He had more chins than Niagara has falls, and they were almost as wet. He mopped at his face with a white handkerchief that could have doubled as a sail for a small ship. He caught my eye and said, 'I could use a drink.' I took my mouth away from the mask and gave another of my wry smiles. I saw him press the button for the stewardess, but nobody came. Had the entire crew parachuted to safety? Eventually the captain turned on his intercom. There was the sound of ragged, heavy breathing. Was he having some sort of seizure?

'This is your captain. We are . . .', then more ragged breathing. Meanwhile, I filled in the gaps. I am a dramatist, after all. I might be a discredited and reviled one, but I am still able to dramatize. I imagined the captain barely alive, the co-pilot dead.

The captain finally managed to control himself. 'There is a fault with the cabin pressure,' he said, 'and also with the oxygen supply.' We would be making a fast descent to 10,000 feet and would then fly over the sea to jettison our fuel. 'For an emergency landing,' groaned the fattest man in Australia. The wobbly descent lasted long enough for me to write an overwrought and dramatic letter of farewell to my family, and for the fattest man in Australia to struggle out of his seat and help himself, me and Mr Grey Suit to a miniature gin. We didn't bother with the ice and lemon. After ditching its fuel the plane flew shakily back to Melbourne and landed, escorted by emergency vehicles.

In the transit lounge I asked an airport official if a small section could be roped off so that the thirty or so smokers on the flight could light up and repair their jangled nerves. 'No,' she said severely. 'It's the Health and Safety rules.' I gave a wry smile.

Grandma at Large

I don't claim to be a good parent. Far from it. I've made many mistakes and I'm still making them. In fact I'm now making mistakes as a grandparent. I recently tried to encourage my grandson Niall into developing a passion for stamp-collecting. I bought the poor boy a bag of mixed stamps from Australia. Under my dictatorship he spent one night of a recent weekend visit sorting the stamps into little piles. There was a Koala pile and a Kangaroo pile and a Famous Aussie Athletes pile. The next night he was encouraged to stick the stamps into a stamp album – I was quite strict about how exactly he stuck the stamps in.

The boy did as he was told, but I could see that he wanted to ask 'Why? What is the purpose of this mindless, repetitive activity, Grandma?' He politely kept his mouth shut, but when I suggested that he might have had enough, he jumped down from the table and was in the other room watching television before you could say 'koala'. His sister, the five-year-old blonde bombshell, was already in there drinking a cocktail and watching *Lolita* on the television. (Before you report me to the NSPCC, let me say that the cocktails consisted of virulently coloured pop, ice, a drinking straw, a plastic palm tree, a monkey on a stick and a paper umbrella; and as for *Lolita*, I've seen more eroticism in *Skippy the Bush Kangaroo*.)

It was very late when we retired for the night. The bombshell wanted to sleep in my bed because (according to her) there is a ghost that lives on the upstairs landing of my house. I was too tired to give her a talk on the lack of statistical evidence as to the existence of paranormal phenomena.

In the morning, they took advantage of me and forced me to agree to take them to see the film *Muppet Treasure Island*. Later I watched them enthusiastically pour cereal into their bowls. I stood by with the milk and sugar bowl. 'We do our own milk and sugar,' they both said indignantly, so I left them to it. When I turned round again I saw that each child had a small mountain of sugar on the top of their cereal. Kilimanjaro sprang to mind. 'How *could* you?' I cried.

'I just *said* not too much sugar, didn't I?' 'But it's not too much sugar for us,' they said reasonably.

We took a taxi to the cinema. On the way, my grandson asked me in a loud voice several difficult questions about the solar system. The taxi driver laughed in a horrible, sneery way at my inept replies. He dropped us off at one of those dreary out-of-town leisure and entertainment complexes. As I looked around at the dull, low, red-brick buildings, I felt a deep loathing for the whole idea of formalized leisure and entertainment, and an urgent need to be at home reading a book. We went to a restaurant before the film started. But when I say restaurant, I want you to know that I use the term very loosely.

We stood obediently by a sign that said 'Please wait to

be seated', but after a few minutes of being ignored by the teenage waiting staff, we got bored and made our own way to a table. We studied the menu. Half an hour later, after much changing of minds and heated discussion among the three of us, a youth arrived with a hand-held computer to take our order. He apologized cheerfully for the delay. 'Nobody knows what they're doing, we're all nutters,' he added, nodding towards his colleagues who were larking about round the serving hatch.

The bombshell's choice, a jacket potato with cheese, drew a shake of the youth's head. 'Not after three o'clock,' he said. I wondered for a moment if a new law had been passed while I'd been out of the country. Was there now a curfew on baked potatoes?

My grandson gave his drink order: 'A chocolate milk-shake, please, extra thick so that the straw stands up in it by itself.' I was proud of his attention to detail, and sad for him when the drink eventually came and the straw needed help to sit down, let alone stand up. The food was unbelievably vile and I now understood why so much of it littered the restaurant floor.

When the youth came to take our almost full plates away, he asked with a gormless smile, 'Everything all right?' 'No, it was horrible,' I said pleasantly. Equally pleasantly he replied, 'We're always busy on Sundays.' Still pleasantly I said, 'We won't be coming back on any day of the week.'

We filled up on popcorn and cola in the cinema. For the next ninety minutes I watched sourly as Kermit and Miss Piggy now cavorted about on Treasure Island, but I did turn every now and again to watch my grandchildren's lovely faces as they stared at the screen. I was happy to be there with them. And I vowed to myself that I would be a better grandmother. I would read them Robert Louis Stevenson's masterpiece, *Treasure Island*, when we got home. I would put the damn stamp album away, I would scare the ghost from the upstairs landing and, finally, I would put three potatoes in the oven to bake.

The Tourist

This is how he died. He went to Maria's Taverna for his usual coffee. Then he went to the fields to see his sheep, he called into his shop, went home feeling unwell, sat on the sofa and died.

The last time I saw the grocer alive was when I went into his long, dark shop to buy some of those blue tablets that slot into a plug-in anti-mosquito device, a tin of evaporated milk and a gaudy pink and white beach mat. He darted about as he always did, muttering in Greek; his voice sounded like rusty nails. There was no price label on the beach mat, nor on any of the other similar mats in the shop. He shouted something to a female in the back room and the female shouted back. To English ears it sounded as though they were having a marriage-ending quarrel, but I knew that all he had probably said to her was 'How much are the pink and white beach mats?' And that her reply to him had probably been, 'I don't know, love.'

Everything about him was bony: his nose, his forehead and his limbs – his elbows could have cut cheese. I don't speak any Greek, apart from the essential pleasantries, so he mimed bafflement, bringing his shoulder blades up to his ears. I mimed back that I would pay what he asked: on the island of Skyros it is taken for granted that everyone is honest.

He went behind the battered shop counter and dragged a fat, dog-eared book from the shelf window. He rifled through the pages. Eventually he found the page he wanted and ran a thin brown finger down a column. I couldn't help but notice that the date at the top of the page ended 1991. He shook his head and threw the book back under the counter, then he took up the beach mat and examined it minutely again. A moment later he was outside in the street asking passers-by if they knew the price. Old women in black put down their shopping bags crammed with onions and aubergines and examined the beach mat. A small crowd of people gathered, each contributing to the debate. In the end a small boy was ordered to go to the haberdasher's down the hill. He came back with the information that the beach mat would cost me 250 drachmas. The grocer wrote the price out for me on a brown paper bag and I paid him, thanked him and left.

The next time I saw him was two days later, and he was being carried shoulder high in an open coffin. His bony, noble head was surrounded by fresh flowers. Somebody had shaved him and the skin on his face looked unfamiliarly smooth. The grocer's funeral was a big public event in the town of Skyros. He had been a very popular man, so businesses and shops closed for the morning. His daughters and sons hurried from Athens to be there on time (the dead have to be buried within twenty-four hours on Skyros as there are no facilities for storing bodies). Large crowds of grieving townsfolk lined the main street, waiting for the coffin to be processed down the hill towards the graveyard.

Then, walking up the hill came three women and three men; obviously tourists. They looked about them with an air of amusement. One of the women was blonde and wearing shorts and a pink and white gingham bikini top. She was obviously anxious to avoid spoiling her tan with strap marks, so she had left the straps dangling so that her breasts were exposed. She was a truly shocking sight. A friend of mine, a lovely woman in her sixties, crossed the street and spoke politely to the blonde, telling her, 'A funeral is about to take place.' The blonde had a T-shirt hanging from her belt, and my friend indicated to her that she should cover herself. But the blonde (who was English) merely said excitedly to her friends, 'There's going to be a funeral,' and stepped forward to get a better view, so exposing herself even more.

Right until the last moment, when the coffin came into sight, I thought she would relent and put on her T-shirt. But she didn't, and the priest and the boys carrying holy artefacts, the grocer's crying sons and daughters and his friends who had loved him passed by the dumb English tourist who had so little respect for their dead. I watched their eyes flicker towards the shocking patch of pink and white and saw them register their disgust, and I cried behind my sunglasses and wanted to apologize to the grocer's family for the terrible disrespect the Englishwoman had shown towards their small town. When the crowds had dispersed the woman strolled up the street, oblivious to the great insult she had caused the polite and courteous people of Skyros. My one consolation was the sight of her retreating back: the sunburned skin looked red and inflamed and I thought that unless she covered up very soon she could be suffering from agonizing sunburn by that evening. But I wasn't going to warn her. Quite honestly, I hoped she'd burn in hell.

No Ideas

People are always writing to me and asking me where I get my ideas from. I'm tempted to reply (as John Cleese once did), 'I buy them from a little old woman who lives round the corner.'

If only that little old woman existed. I'd be there, outside her door, at the front of the queue, jostling with other desperate writers who have run out of ideas. Because, I'd better come clean, I've no idea what to write for this month's column. It's a grey day in an uninspiring month, nothing particularly interesting has happened to me, I've run out of ideas and I'm bored by my own company. Somebody once said, 'Writing is easy. All you have to do is to stare down at a blank piece of paper until your forehead bleeds.'

You may think this is nonsense, but I think I feel the first trickle of blood. It's not as though I am struggling against any editorial restrictions. If I wanted to say that John Major reminds me of Postman Pat, the trade restrictions imposed by America against Cuba should be lifted, or that schools are wasted on the young, I could say it. The editor is not a despot using his columnists to impose his extreme political views – 'Today Sainsbury's *The Magazine*, tomorrow the world!'

I once went to Russia, before communism became a dirty word, and met a group of government-approved writers. What a sad bunch they were. You could tell that none of them had ever bled from the forehead. I wonder what they are doing for a living now, post-communism? They may well be criminals, crime currently being the growth industry in the country formerly known as Russia.

Good writers and good criminals have quite a lot in common. (By good criminals, I mean in the sense of being good at their job.) Both are inadequates, both give ten per cent of their income to a 'fence' (a writer's fence is called an agent). And both are students of human fallibility. I'm a gormless trusting type myself so I have a foot in both camps. I could easily have fallen for a scam I read about some years ago. It went something like this. In bold black letters it said:

Do you want to be rich beyond your wildest dreams? Of course you do!!!!!

Then, in slightly smaller letters, it went on:

I have a penthouse in London, a villa in Marbella, a powerboat, three high-performance cars. I drink champagne every day. I buy my suits from Savile Row . . .

This boasting continued at tedious length until near the bottom, in large letters, it said:

Yet I only work one day a week!!!!!!

(Incidentally, one exclamation mark is bad enough, but if you see six it's a sure sign that either a teenager or a criminal is behind them.) At the very bottom it said something like:

Send £5. Yes! Only £5! And find out how I finance my fabulous lifestyle. Send to: Rikki Conman, Unit One, Kray Way, Maxwell Industrial Park, Bentchester.

Hundreds of gullible fools sent their cash and cheques and postal orders to Rikki Conman and waited eagerly for his reply. And to be fair to Rikki, his reply came within a couple of weeks. And what did it say? Inside their stamped addressed envelope was a slip of paper on which was written four simple words:

Do as I do.

Diabolically clever, eh? I wonder where Rikki gets his ideas from? I've just got up from the table where I'm trying to work and paced about a bit, like expectant fathers used to do in black-and-white films. My eyes happened to fall on the magazine *Hello!* (note the exclamation mark), which just happened to be on the table because I just happened to have bought it at the garage. I've never bought it before, honest guv, but the cover was irresistible. Prince Edward is standing next to his fiancée, Sophie. He is dressed in a sort of sheet, she is dressed as a knight (though the grey polo-neck she is wearing under her ill-fitting tabard is from Marks & Sparks, or I'm a dingo).

I just happened to turn the pages and discovered that Edward and Sophie were among 1,000 guests at a costume party for a vulgar aristocrat (I won't give him the nitrogen of publicity). It must have been galling for the aristo, that his OTT costume didn't make the front cover, having been designed by an opera supremo and made up by a college of art. How he must have fulminated against the editorial policy that chose dull, sheet-bedecked royalty against mere aristo ostentation.

Anyway, if there are any little old women out there with ideas to sell, I'm in the market. You can tell from this month's column how desperate I am.

Lost Bag

I was wandering around the red-light district in Amsterdam recently, shivering in a cutting wind (British Airways had managed to lose the bag with my warm sweater in it). The scantily dressed girls displaying themselves in the windows had portable heaters at their feet, but were still obviously cold. How they managed to look sultry at the same time is clearly a professional skill passed on to new recruits.

Sometimes, if you looked beyond the girls, you caught a glimpse of the bed where they exercised other skills. I was quite touched at how spartan and clean these beds appeared, and I dreaded to think how much their weekly laundry costs must be. Every bed was made up with white sheets and pillowcases. They looked like nice girls; the type you could take to tea with your old uncle without him becoming over-excited.

Some of the girls were reading books (I think business was slow that night); others had a piece of sewing on their naked laps. One rubber-clad siren was leaning on a tasselled whip, talking and laughing with her friend, who had opted for the baby-doll look (though I have yet to see Hamleys

selling baby dolls wearing white stockings and suspenders).
It was all strangely innocent.

Window shopping in the red-light district becomes
monotonous after a while. There are identical goods for
sale: the same pink plastic phalluses, the same bottles of
love potions for ingestion or application, and the same
seven-inch black patent stilettos. I was almost tempted to
buy a pair of these shoes (my own high heels were in the
bag with the warm sweater, in the care of BA). I was sick
of wearing my dumpy training-type shoes. But I came to
my senses. Those cobbles, my dears!

The next day I enquired at the hotel reception desk
whether the lost bags had been returned. I kept my distance
from the receptionist, conscious that by now, after wearing
the same clothes for three days, I must . . . well . . . smell.
'No,' she said. I had already scrounged a toothbrush and
toothpaste from the hotel, but I doubted if they kept an
emergency wardrobe for guests parted from their luggage.
There was only one thing for it. I had to buy new clothes.
And it would be that rare thing, guilt-free shopping!

It was a moment of pure happiness. I shuffled my credit
cards excitedly and set off for the shops. My spirits damp-
ened slightly when I saw that the pavement was lined with
beggars. I gave generously of my guilders, but being exposed
to so much human misery took the edge off my euphoria.
So when I passed through the revolving doors into the
perfumed warmth of a department store, some of the guilt
had returned.

I made my way up to Women's Clothing on the second
floor, and was immediately plunged into a nightmare of
choice. Rack upon rack of lovely clothes stretched into the
far distance, and I swear, dear reader, I examined every size

label, every price tag of every garment that I would even consider wearing. When I glanced at my watch I couldn't believe the time. I had obviously fallen into some kind of retail black hole, wandered into another dimension: two hours had passed, and I was still wearing my stinking three-day-old clothes.

Exhausted and confused, I made my way to a café on the same floor. It was full of women like me. We wore that distracted look, the one that says that we are mentally cataloguing the old clothes in our wardrobes at home.

I don't speak or read Dutch, but I know that the first item on a Dutch menu is always the soup. So I pointed to the top of the menu when the waitress came, and settled back to more mental gymnastics. Would the orange padded waistcoat I'd seen go under the black leather jacket? Etc., etc . . .

The soup came in a bowl as big as a Belisha beacon. It was full of meatballs and dumplings, and every vegetable grown on the earth. It was served with a foot and a half of French bread. I thanked her, but she hadn't finished. She came back and put down a dinner plate covered in wedges of international cheeses (I swear one was Red Leicester), then she placed a salad bowl, big enough to bath a baby in, on the table. Next came a three-storey apple cake and a jug of cream. The final item was the only one I was pleased to see: a large glass of champagne.

When she saw my alarm (what was coming next? A boar's head? A roast ox?) she explained in halting English that I had ordered the set lunch. When her back was turned I shovelled some of the cheese into my handbag, but the table was still groaning, and what was meant to be a ten-minute stop to think turned into a forced-feed lasting an hour.

I went back into the shop and bought the orange padded waistcoat. It fits under the jacket, but it isn't warm, it doesn't cover my bum and when I got back to England and looked out of the train I saw a whole lot of Railtrack maintenance men in orange waistcoats similar to mine. Too similar. I blame British Airways.

Christmas in Tobago

I know it's April, but I didn't tell you about my Christmas in Tobago. We packed our suitcases during a Christmas party (immediate family only – nobody else could have tolerated the juxtaposition of mince pies and mosquito repellent on the table).

In the preceding week I'd finished the first draft of a new book, rewritten a film script and Christmas-shopped until I was completely demented. It was a peculiar party: my sister nobly ironed my holiday clothes while I opened my Christmas presents – a huge straw hat from one daughter, a sarong from another.

The departure hall at Gatwick was reminiscent of those medieval paintings depicting Hell, where tormented souls mill around for eternity. Nobody actually poked us with a three-pronged fork, but they fed us misinformation followed by no information until we were in a state of total dependency, like the cowed population of a totalitarian state. If I was in charge of Gatwick airport, I would lay on complimentary drinks for those in the check-in queues, and some sort of live entertainment. Actors could join the queue and stage a scripted family row – something meaty that would keep us all riveted until it was our turn to reach the check-in desk and discover that our passports were at home on top of the fridge.

We queued on the aircraft steps in a wind so cold that it was painful to open our eyes. When I opened mine, I half expected to see a polar bear in front of me, shivering. Eight hours later we walked off a different set of steps in Tobago to the feel of sunshine and the sound of *Jingle Bells* played on steel drums. Smiling Tobagonian women greeted us with complimentary Carib beer, which we were allowed to take with us inside the arrivals hall. Staid English men and women began to sway their creaky hips, and memories of Gatwick fell away.

I was there to work, running a writing course. The hours were not arduous – three hours a morning, five days a week, and the people on the course were delightful and talented, which made the 'work' easier. The classes could hardly have been more informal. Half of us lay around on sunbeds, others sat on those white plastic chairs that are slowly taking over the world. The terrace was shady, and instead of a coffee break we would stop for cold beer and a dip in the pool. We made each other laugh and, once again, I was thrilled with the standard of writing people were able to achieve with only a little encouragement and a very short deadline. There was plenty to write about: Tobago is extraordinarily beautiful. It is mountainous, with an interior rainforest and an astonishing variety of trees. The climate is wonderfully varied, and within half an hour there can be hot sunshine, billowing cloud, then torrential rain. So the British were able to indulge in their favourite topic of conversation, the weather.

My husband hired the worst Jeep on the island: there were holes in the floor (air conditioning, he said), a resident lizard and nonexistent suspension. I asked him if, as he drove away, he had heard loud laughter coming from inside the car-hire office. 'No,' he said. 'They were already laughing when I got there.' This may have had something to do with the fact that his straw hat had taken on a peculiar shape during the flight and now looked like something Miss Marple might jam on her head while snooping around a vicar's tea party.

We had some thrilling drives on the steep, potholed roads. Every few seconds brought something to delight the eye: deserted beaches, a pretty cow tethered to a notice that said, 'It is forbidden to tether cows here,' a hummingbird, pelicans diving for fish, children waving.

Tobago is a developing country, and piped water is still a luxury in some places. Many people were filling containers from roadside taps before lugging them up hills to where they lived. Music was everywhere. The remotest village seemed to have a sound system more suited to the acoustics of the Royal Albert Hall than the small shacks it emanated from.

We were warned in the official tourist guide not to pick up hitchhikers, but we ignored this advice. Almost the first lift we gave was to a wild-eyed man wielding a machete on his way to farm coconuts. Another hitchhiker was a fireman on his way to work fifteen miles from his village. We took a young mother and her small baby to Scarborough, the capital, so that she could ask the baby's father to pay his maintenance or go to jail for two weeks.

The finest asset Tobago has is its people. Their kindness, good humour and lovely manners impressed me so much that I want to go back – soon. Like on the next plane.

The Kitchen with
the Mobiles

It's the damned kitchen's fault that we're thinking about moving. We've lived in it for fifteen years without finishing the building work or decorating it. So because the kitchen is in limbo it has become a repository for junk furniture and kitsch ornaments. The latest acquisition is a blow-up three-foot-high model of Munch's 'The Scream', which I won in a raffle. This hideous-looking thing terrified the grandchildren at first, though they quickly got used to it, and the babies now greet it with an airy wave. It does take strangers by surprise, though. We had a policeman visit us recently (don't ask), and I saw him flinch when he looked up from his notebook to see 'The Scream' looming over him from its place next to the fridge.

The kitchen ceiling is hung with mobiles that the children have bought over the years. The last one came from Tenerife in August 1996 and consists of about thirty wooden parrots, all painted in primary colours. There is an over-stuffed bookcase, toy boxes, a sofa and two cluttered dressers. My eldest son, looking round at the kitchen, said, 'This room contains more objects than are known to man.'

This morning I resolved to clear some of the objects away. I walked round the kitchen with an empty cardboard box, picked up a small bottle from one of the dressers, unscrewed the top and sniffed. 'Mind if I throw this aftershave away?' I asked my husband. 'Yes,' he said. 'That aftershave is actually ginger liqueur I brought back from Tobago.'

This disheartened me a bit and reminded me that my eyesight is deteriorating rapidly. I no longer laugh at the cartoons of poor Mr Magoo as he bumbles around. I am now Mrs Magoo, who wonders why she can't get a lather with the new shampoo before realizing it's the conditioner. I've had a near miss with the depilatory cream as well. I once got as far as squeezing it on to my toothbrush before realizing my mistake. I haven't yet applied toothpaste to my underarms, but I know the day will come. Why don't manufacturers use bold black letters on their potions? And isn't it about time somebody invented wipers on spectacles so that you could wear your specs in the bath? I'd do it myself, but I'm a bit busy.

Anyway, back to the damn kitchen. It's where everybody sits. People like its comfortable eccentricity. But I don't any more. I now admire minimalism, I want to move into a beautiful, empty house, with just a few essential items of furniture.

The kitchen in this fantasy house would have a stark look. The only decorative piece allowed would be a large modern painting. Carefully chosen cooking equipment would be displayed in severe lines on a shelf. The only things suspended from the ceiling would be halogen lights illuminating the empty work surfaces. The thirty garish parrots would have to roost somewhere else. Children's toys would be banished, as would novelty lamps, Elvis Presley clocks, plastic tulips, the odd-sock bag and the sofa. The cat would be allowed in, but only because he would fit in with the colour scheme (he's black and white), but his basket and feeding bowls would be out.

I can see myself moving around in this starkly simplistic white space, wearing elegant black or white clothes, preparing simple yet nutritious meals for the family. Of course the family wouldn't be in this kitchen, arguing and scoffing at *The Archers* and reading the papers and dripping ice-lolly juice on the white floor and helping themselves to the fruit bowl. They would have fled, taking the Elvis clock and the parrots with them.

My new kitchen wouldn't have a fruit bowl, of course; all those clashing fruit colours – ugh! So, as I said, we're possibly on the move.

My husband has given the local estate agents a laugh by faxing them with our requirements. I quote: 'The property will have water: lake/river/pond/stream/brook, and will be surrounded by mixed woodland.'

I'm guessing now, but I think my husband's fantasy is of tramping through the mixed woodland with a boxer dog by his side. I asked him when he was at his lowest ebb recently (it was 3.30 in the morning) if he would truly, madly, deeply like a dog, and he roused himself and rhapsodized about the virtues of the boxer breed. So in his fantasy he's walking through our woods on his way to admire our lake/river/pond/stream/brook, while I'm in the white kitchen stirring something pale on the hi-tech stove and waiting for his return. This is where our fantasies collide, because I couldn't possibly allow a drooling, muddy-pawed dog into my fantasy kitchen. No – the boxer would have to live outside in a minimalist kennel, with a Conran feeding bowl.

None of this will happen, of course. We'll still be sitting in the same kitchen this time next year, with 'The Scream' and the Elvis clock and the thirty hanging parrots.

Idling

I needed to go somewhere to work on the third draft of a book, *A Man Walking His Dog*. I have a workroom at home and an office two miles away from home, but I find it increasingly difficult to work in either of these places (people tend to drop in for a chat). I need to go alone, to a place where nobody knows me, where I can sit outside and work crazy hours. Which is why I ended up in Barbados recently.

I went to a travel agent and said I needed to go somewhere hot for fourteen days. He pressed a couple of buttons on his computer and Barbados came up straight away. The cost of a return ticket was £300. 'I'll take it,' I said. It was a record transaction.

Days before I'd been slagging the place off. My husband and I had been trapped in transit in Barbados airport on the way back from Tobago. Other passengers spent their time buying emeralds and queuing for food and drink. I spent mine wanting a cigarette (a thousand curses on airports that won't give us smokers our own small, smoky corner).

I wasn't too impressed by the English visitors to Barbados. True, I only saw them from behind glass, but there seemed to be a high percentage of colonel and the colonel's lady types. One couple, he in a blazer despite the searing heat, she in a Laura Ashley frock and hat, actually did walk with their noses in the air. They may have both suffered from a rare medical condition that necessitated keeping their nostrils uplifted – if so I'm sorry for them – but the impression they gave as they walked behind their porter, who was pushing their enormous pile of luggage, was of the snooty English abroad.

I vowed never to go. I have a horror of places where such types congregate. I imagine being trapped with them: him in the hotel bar telling his interminable army stories and her confessing to me on the beach that he's a callous brute and she longs to leave him. None of this could happen in reality, of course, because when I go on holiday I never speak to anybody apart from bar staff and waiters (and, of course, my husband, if he's with me).

Anyroad up, as they say in Leicester, I went to Barbados to work. On my return, people asked me what it was like. 'I don't know,' I had to reply. I saw the immediate environs of my hotel, the Shangri-La, and perhaps a mile of exquisite beach, and that was it. I was in my room by half past six each night, cowering from the mosquitoes and preparing a meal of corned beef, vegetable rice and pineapple. I spent the rest of the evening sitting up in bed rewriting my book.

Each morning I went shopping for more corned beef, vegetables etc., at the poorly stocked supermarket, which was in sight of the hotel. However, although it was not far, this was not a simple journey – there were obstacles on the way. On the opposite side of the road was a huge tree with a thick trunk on which was written in white paint, 'No idlers'. In the shade of the tree on a low wall sat a collection of idlers, youngish good-looking men. The wall was stony, so they had brought along bum-sized pieces of foam to make idling more comfortable. On spying a woman walking alone, they would invite her to sit next to them and whip out another piece of foam. If you declined the foam and carried on walking, they would run after you and entreat you to 'chill out, woman'.

They would wave the piece of foam intended for you in the air enticingly, as though it were a priceless piece of gold cloth. I have to tell you that many single British women 'took the foam' and were later to be seen buying the various idlers drinks and meals in the hotels on the sea shore. I can only speculate on what happened at night because, as I've said, I was in my room, eating my corned beef and rice and my tinned pineapple. (Yes, all on the same plate; the conventions tend to break down when you're on your own.)

It was a damned nuisance at the time, running the gauntlet of the idlers, but they were never offensive and I must admit that some of their shouted remarks were quite nice.

'Hey, Susan!' (Yes, I cracked and told them my name.)

'Hey, I like the way you walk, woman.' And, 'You got style, woman.' But the words that stay uppermost in my mind are those spoken by the chief idler, Peter.

'You should sit down and chill for a while, Susan. There's more to life than work, y'know.'

Display Models

I was watching the local news on television recently (usually a comically gruesome experience). There was an item on, specifically to do with Leicester, and film was shown purporting to be of Leicester citizens being interviewed in Leicester city-centre street. But eagle-eyed Townsend spotted that it wasn't a Leicester street in the film, it was a Nottingham street. All our city centres look alike. The only landmark that especially distinguishes Leicester is its clock tower, and any day now I expect to see that it has been turned into a security watch-tower, with guards posted on the ramparts ready to turn anybody in who has been spotted singing or smoking or laughing in the street. It is a joyless business being a consumer – knowing that the only reason you're wanted in the city centre is for your money.

My washing machine has been broken for two weeks now. Dirty clothing is stacked like planes over Heathrow, but I can't bring myself to enter a shop and be told, yet again, that they have only the display model in stock. And that, even though the porthole door has been yanked open a thousand times and that the switches have been pressed and the detergent tray has been dragged open, I cannot have a discount. I like to take my goods away on the day I pay for them, I am unable to wait for items to be delivered from the John o'Groat's warehouse. In recent months, I have bought a rice cooker, a toaster, a television and a video, all of them display models. Is this an incredible coincidence or have the big electrical chains secretly done away with their stock rooms?

I recently selected a mobile phone from the display cabinet in a large store. The salesman said, 'I'll just check that we've got one in stock.' Smiling pleasantly, I said, 'You won't have one, you'll come back and tell me that I'll have to buy the display model.' In a very short time he was back saying . . . Well, you know what he said, I can't be bothered to write it down.

So I'm washing by hand. My husband has made valiant attempts to mend the washing machine (which broke two weeks after the warranty expired). He has even converted a brass picture hook into a washer for the nut that attaches some damn thing to the belt that turns the drum around. But despite his best efforts, the home-made washer refused to bond with the nut. The grown-up children who live in this house did a lot of cynical eye-rolling as they watched my husband grit his teeth and wrench the back off the washing machine, yet again. They live in an age of built-in obsolescence.

I blame myself for not setting a good example – the last time I darned a sock was about the time of the moon landings. But there is a certain pleasure to be had in washing by hand and hanging it out in the garden. I get great pleasure in watching the wet washing billow and crack on the line in a stiff breeze. Though, it has to be said, I get more pleasure from a large vodka tonic. I now get out of bed in the morning and hope for wind, rather like the captain of a becalmed sailing ship.

When the children were young, I couldn't afford a washing machine. I used to fill the bath with warm water and biological washing powder and encourage my child labourers to stamp up and down on the clothes. The scene was something out of Dickens. But the children seemed to enjoy it (we didn't have a television either) and it didn't half get their feet clean. Once the washing had been pegged out on the line, it often used to hang there for three or four days. Once it was unpegged and brought into the house, it immediately transformed itself into that monstrous thing called the ironing. I wonder how many people ever get to the bottom of their ironing basket. I know I've got something (it's a blouse of some kind, composed of polka dots and frills) that has been lurking in the basket since Cliff Richard won the Eurovision Song Contest.

I hate all of my domestic appliances. The vacuum cleaner has a mad fit and chokes to death if asked to suck up anything bigger than a baby's fingernail clipping; the iron is menopausal and has hot flushes and scorches linen; the dishwasher maliciously coats everything in diluted mashed potatoes; and the tumble dryer doesn't believe in interfering with nature and, after an hour of noisy tumbling, returns the washing as wet as when it was first put in.

I know I'll give in eventually and drag myself out to a dreary, windswept retail park and buy myself a new washing machine. If you hear about the salesman who was attacked by a middle-aged woman for saying 'I'm afraid we've only got the display model, madam', you'll know it was me.

Giving Advice

At my elbow, as I write, is a slithering pile of unanswered letters. At least half of them are from school children who have been encouraged by their teachers to write to an author. These children are doing projects and have specific questions to which they need answers. Most of their enquiries are pretty routine: How long did it take you?; Where do you get your ideas from? etc. But occasionally I get asked, Do you have any advice?

I hate getting advice myself. If I'm about to embark on a foolish adventure in a strange place with dubious strangers, the last thing I want is somebody advising me to stay at home and be sensible. I try never to give advice myself. People resent it. I've lost track of the times I've urged women to leave their moronic, bullying, mean-spirited, lazy husbands. These women have sobbed pitifully as they've recounted the daily horrors of living with the beast. But when I've said 'Leave him', they've looked resentful and said, 'How can I? I love him', and gone home and ironed his vile underpants.

Just as useless is to give advice to your own children: I

think there is possibly a physiological problem of the auditory canal that affects children on their thirteenth birthday. I have observed this phenomenon many times.

What happens is this . . . the parent talks, giving advice to the child about education, clothes, choice of friends, etc., and a device – a flap of skin, perhaps – falls down inside the inner ears and blocks out all sound. The parent carries on talking (responsible sex . . . blah . . . condom . . . blah . . . say no to drugs . . . blah, blah, blah . . .) and the child nods, and appears to be listening, but does not hear a word.

Another group immune to advice are male cooks, who regard herbs and spices as a substitute for testosterone. If a recipe calls for one bay leaf, they fling in six. If Delia suggests a few sprigs of rosemary, they will uproot the bush and throw it on to the roast lamb – root, soil and all. It is useless to protest; they will accuse you of cramping their style and order you out of your own kitchen.

Gardeners are also impervious to sensible advice. I once heard a woman at a garden centre ask a wizened old expert plantsman if she could grow lavender in deep shade. 'No, no,' he said, and gave her a long list of plants to whom shade is heaven. 'I'll try it anyway,' she said, and picked up fifteen quid's worth of doomed lavender.

People are constantly giving me advice, urging me to slow down, not to work so hard. In the same breath, paradoxically, they try to encourage me to go to the gym to work out.

I've got a fear of gymnasiums. It stems from school, when we hefty girls with puppy fat thighs were expected to heave ourselves over the vaulting horse whilst wearing hideous navy-blue knickers: possibly the most unflattering garment ever worn. And country dancing took place in the gym.

To the sound of some scratchy 'hey nonny no' 78 rpm record, we girls would be forced to dance in the style of village maidens. The music was innocent, but most of us girls were not. We smouldered with love for Elvis, and sported beehive hairdos and had read certain pages in *Lady Chatterley's Lover*.

If ever the sequences in country dancing broke down, it was inevitably my fault. I've always had a problem following instructions. Our gym teacher – a stocky woman in an Aertex top and flared gym knickers – would bellow the various moves at me, but I couldn't get my feet to follow. I would 'hey' when I was meant to be 'nonnying'.

So I won't be joining a gym. I'll take my exercise as I've always taken it. It's called walking the streets and it has the marvellous advantage that I can look at people's gardens and peer through their front windows.

There is one piece of advice I have always given and will continue to give: read books. Books are cheap (second hand), are entertaining, enlightening, portable and don't need batteries.

William Brown

My husband has just returned from a trip to Iceland. He enthused about the natural and man-made wonders of the place: the geysers that spurt hot water into the air at regular intervals; the ancient glaciers; the fact that a large beer costs £10 a glass. However, it was when he told me that 99 per cent of the Icelandic population are literate that I got excited. If Icelandic schools can produce such spectacular results, why can't ours in Britain? According to the Basic Skills Agency, one in six people in Britain has literacy problems.

I think we are entitled to ask why so many children are leaving school (after eleven years of compulsory education) unable to read and write their own language satisfactorily. I was once told by a middle-class, highly literate woman that: 'Reading and writing isn't everything. We should learn to value people for themselves, they have other skills.' We were in a literacy centre at the time, full of adults struggling, with the help of their tutors, to learn their own language. A couple of people were in their seventies and had spent a lifetime covering up the fact that they couldn't read or write. Some of their excuses were ingenious. One man wrapped a bandage around his right hand whenever he had an official form to fill in. Other, more common, excuses are: 'I've forgotten my glasses' or 'I've lost my contact lenses' or 'My handwriting is bad'.

I was a late reader myself, so I can empathize with the terror of looking down at a page full of incomprehensible black squiggles. I used to dread being asked to read by the teacher in my infant school (who was so unkind and sadistic that my brain turned to porridge whenever I saw her). I learned to read during an absence from school. I was away for three weeks with mumps (incidentally, what happened to mumps? They seem to have been phased out, along with impetigo and growing pains). My mother bought Richmal Crompton's *Just William* books from a rummage sale, and I was so captivated by the ink drawings that I wanted to know what the captions said underneath. My mother read them to me, and somehow, by the time I went back to school, I could read the books myself.

For those of you who don't know the William books, I'd better explain their attraction. They start in the 1930s when William Brown is an eleven-year-old boy (he never gets older, though he is always having birthdays). He lives in a village in the country with his family. His mother, Mrs Brown, is a long-suffering woman prone to headaches. Mrs Brown can't quite bring herself to think badly of William, though God knows there is daily evidence that he is the son from hell. Mr Brown is a permanently angry man. He catches a train to the city each weekday. Unlike his wife, he is convinced that William is the spawn of the devil. The village policeman frequently greets Mr Brown on his return home.

William leads a gang called 'The Outlaws', but he is not

a wicked boy. Although it has to be admitted that his catalogue of crimes – breaking and entering, kidnapping, forgery, arson – would put him in the care of the social services today. In fact, he'd probably be locked away in a secure unit for criminally insane children. The books are wonderfully subversive and have a rich, sophisticated vocabulary. The reader sees the adult world through William's eyes and, like him, finds it a baffling, hypocritical place.

William Brown hated school and was constantly in trouble. And, judging by the letters he wrote (ransom notes, usually), he struggled with his spelling and punctuation. My literary hero never grew up, but I hope that a good teacher out there in Fictionland persevered with him and that he left school able to read and write. Because I fear that William's 'other skills' – subversion, hand-to-hand fighting – would not have adequately equipped him for adult life. Unless, of course, he wanted to join the foreign legion, whose only entry qualification is that applicants must have four limbs.

Good teachers should be venerated by society. We should pay them more and stop being jealous of their long holidays. Boring, inadequate teachers should be sifted out before they leave teacher-training college. On no account should their malign influence be allowed to pollute the lives of small children. One of my daughters wept every night for weeks because she was afraid of the 'shouting' teacher.

Millions of jobs have disappeared now, and will never return. However, unemployed people remain, and it's only fair that if they are to stay at home in enforced idleness, they should be allowed to pick up a book and be able to read it.

Stonehenge

Stonehenge has always fascinated me. I first visited it when I was twelve years old. In those days it was possible to wander amongst the stones and, shock-horror, actually touch them. People used to picnic inside the stone circle and at night, according to the *News of the World*, less innocent activities took place.

It's very different today; Stonehenge now has a Visitor Centre run by English Heritage. It is all very tasteful and controlled and unsatisfactory. There is a chain-link fence separating the nearby road from the site, so the only way to get reasonably close to the stones is to pay £3.75 to a bored teenager in a green shed and pass through a turnstile that leads to a tunnel under the road. Inside the tunnel there is a huge collection of what look like mobile phones, decorated in flags of the world. My husband rummaged through them and eventually found the Union Jack. He pressed 'play' and a gentleman with the type of English tea-planter accent rarely heard today, started to bark information about Stonehenge through a background noise of feedback whine and static.

We passed by a mural painted on the walls of the tunnel that depicted primitive man dragging the stones across the plains. I hate to be muralist, but quite honestly this painting looked as though primitive man himself had dipped a stick into various substances – swamp water, sheep dung, animal blood – and daubed it, er . . . primitively, on to the wall. We emerged to find the stones bathed in sunlight and casting shadows on the spongy bright green grass surrounding them.

The stones were encircled by a low rope and I had an irresistible urge to jump over this symbolic barrier and run towards the circle. But, not wishing to be dragged away by English Heritage guards in front of an international audience with cameras, I resisted the urge and continued to shuffle along behind the other tourists. We switched the tea planter off toot-sweet. He was mostly incomprehensible but the little we did hear sounded as though Barbara Cartland and Shakespeare had collaborated on his script. No wonder the Americans looked baffled.

We made slow progress. Every few steps we had to stop so as not to spoil somebody's photo or video opportunity. I rarely take a camera anywhere with me now. To me, a camera is just one more damned thing to lose, or have stolen. I know that in my old age I'll regret not being able to turn the pages of a photo album and conjure up those magic moments in my life. But I'm banking on still having a memory. If I close my eyes I can still see those magnificent stones (though I have to admit that it was only last week).

We went back down the tunnel and walked past the gift shop. My husband clutched at my arm. 'Aren't you well?' he said. 'You've passed the gift shop.' I looked in the window and saw a heap of small teddy bears dressed in scraps of mock leopard skin, representing primitive man, I presume. In another window were other bears wearing English Heritage sweaters complete with the yellow badge. There should be a society for the protection of teddy bears. They are grossly exploited by the tourist industry. They have to work in shocking conditions with the stink of potpourri in their woollen nostrils and the sound of electronic cash tills ringing in their ears.

I followed my husband reluctantly into the shop. He was in a generous mood. 'Do you want a pair of Stonehenge earrings?' he asked solicitously. I smiled a wintry smile and refused his kind offer. There were long queues at the tills. A Japanese woman was obviously intending to lug five jars of Olde English jam back to Japan. A fat American man had bought a giant Stonehenge lollipop, which he looked at greedily and would probably scoff in his hotel room later that night. I left the shop empty handed, which I considered to be a milestone in my personal development. My goal in life is to buy only what I need. Unfortunately I still need rather a lot.

Later we sat on a picnic bench overlooking a fenced-off field full of sheep. One sheep headed off into the distance and the others followed – apart from one which stuck its head through the fence. Sheep are famously stupid, but this one looked like an imbecile and was incredibly ugly. But before you could say Little Bo Peep the woolly imbecile was surrounded by a phalanx of tourists videoing and photographing its ugly mug. I swear that sheep thought it was Princess Diana. It was clearly addicted to fame, because it wasn't until the tourists got back into their coaches that it dragged itself away from the fence and went to join the other sheep at the far end of the field.

Horrible Supermarket

A new supermarket (*not* Sainsbury's) opened near me recently. I was away at the time, but my children, who are at the cutting edge of grocery shopping, had already visited. They warned me to dress warmly. It was a sweltering day, the sun was an oxyacetylene torch directed on Leicester, but I obeyed and wore a cardigan, trousers and a shirt. I was accompanied by my granddaughter, Fin, who is two years old, and her father.

We got out of the car. Fin said, 'Look . . . dinosaur,' in a matter-of-fact kind of voice, as though dinosaurs make a habit of hanging around supermarket car parks on a Saturday afternoon. But the kid was right. There was a dinosaur tethered to a bike rack, as if its prehistoric owner had nipped inside for a stoneground loaf.

Round the corner strolled a twelve-foot-high man. Fin looked up at him with unblinking eyes. 'Hello,' he said, tipping his top hat to her. 'Hello, man,' she said, unfazed by his weird stilt legs. A little white dog, wearing a tartan bow tie and a bowler hat, was lapping water from a bowl near the entrance doors. Fin watched it gravely. By now I was wondering if there would be Martians stacking the shelves, or gorillas on the checkouts and, if this was the case, would Fin accept it as part of normal supermarket shopping. Then I reminded myself that all two-year-olds are mad. It's part of their cranky charm. Fin's most prized possession at the moment is a postcard of a grinning pig looking through a window.

We proceeded inside to find Antarctica: blinding white light and low temperatures. If a flock of penguins had wandered down the aisle towards us, I would not have been surprised. I pulled my cardigan around me and looked in pity at other shoppers, most of whom were shivering in their singlets and shorts. Some crazed women were wearing bikini tops, as though they'd just ambled off a beach.

I think a supermarket lives or falls on the freshness of its fruit and vegetables, and this one fell a very long way. It was a veritable bungee jump of rotten tomatoes and withered corn on the cob. I snatched the last bunch of sad-looking salad onions and eavesdropped on a conversation between two suited managers who were congratulating themselves on their first week's turnover. Their backs were turned to a mound of soft potatoes which were sprouting ominous green shoots. The phrase 'fiddling while Rome burns' sprang to mind.

My temples began to throb, which is always a sign that I am going to *say something*. My children used to dread these occasions. One daughter still shudders at my asking yobs on a bus to stop swearing (they didn't; their language just got worse, and the other passengers looked at me resentfully, as if *I* were the one with the foul mouth).

I pushed the trolley away from the smug managers and the smell of rotten fruit and veg, and inspected the fresh meat counter. I asked a friendly looking youth if he had any lamb's liver. He appeared never to have heard of it. I wondered if it had been phased out, along with half-crown pieces and washing mangles. He offered me pig's liver, but it looked too *much* like offal; too much as if it had only just left the poor pig. I swear it was still *pulsating* on its tray, so I turned it down. By now we'd been in the store for fifteen minutes, but already my hands and feet were icy cold. I longed to abandon the trolley and make a run for the sunshine outside. Fin's cheeks had lost their pretty blush and turned a whiter shade of blue.

But I stuck it out and we proceeded round the store to the checkout, passing the man on stilts who was bent double over the shelves doing his shopping. His basket showed the evidence of a lonely life: frozen dinners for one, a small loaf, a box of dried chow mein.

While Fin was taken on her second visit to the toilet, a boy helped me to pack. I needed his help as I found it impossible to open the flimsy carrier bags. It was temple-throbbing time again. To make conversation, I asked him if he was cold in his short-sleeved shirt. 'I'm used to it now,' he said, with Scott of the Antarctic bravery. But the woman on the checkout told me she was wearing a long-sleeved thermal vest underneath her overall. 'Everybody's complaining about the cold in here,' she confided.

I thought about the unfriendly temperature, the rotten tomatoes, the smug managers and the impossible-to-open carrier bags, and considered throwing myself down on to the floor and having a two-year-old-type tantrum, but I restrained myself. Fin was back from the toilet and she wouldn't have approved.

Stupid Susan/ Sensible Susan

A Nervous Breakdown for Christmas

(A duologue)

The cast is as follows (in order of appearance):
Stupid Susan – a woman in her fifties (a smoker)
Sensible Susan – a woman in her fifties (a non-smoker)

[*Stupid Susan is sorting through a bowl of earrings, trying to find two the same – a hopeless task.*]

STUPID SUSAN [*to herself*]: So, I'm at home in Leicester this Christmas, stuffing the turkey's bum. Perhaps weeping over the damn thing [*she sighs*] as I remember last Christmas Day spent on a beach in Tobago. Did I really drink champagne in a warm, turquoise sea, or was it a fantastical dream? Did my husband finally learn to dance to the amplified sound of a steel band, or did I only imagine us swaying together in rhythmic harmony on a dance floor for the first time in twenty-two years? The maintenance problems at the hotel have been forgiven, if not forgotten. The shower that burst into flames, the electricity failures, the water supply with a will of its own. I didn't mind any of these inconveniences, though I have to admit that I was not the woman in the flaming shower. She may find it harder to forgive. Our Christmas table may have a Caribbean theme this year.

[*She paces the room, falling off her purple platform slingbacks.*]

Yes, I can see it now, we sit down to a table decorated with tropical flowers. Instead of paper hats we wear sarongs and garlands round our necks. We drink rum punch and eat to the sound of the *Hallelujah Chorus* played on steel drums. I could drag the grandkids' sandpit into the kitchen, throw in some shells, step into it, close my eyes and transport myself to Tobago.

[*Sensible Susan enters.*]

SENSIBLE SUSAN: OK, OK. That's enough, stop right there and take a few deep breaths. No! I didn't mean inhale more deeply on that cigarette – calm yourself, Stupid. You're getting into your usual Christmas panic and taking refuge in ludicrous Caribbean fantasies.

STUPID SUSAN: OK Sensible, so why don't you help me out about Christmas, eh? Why haven't you bought and wrapped the presents by 1 October, and ordered the turkey by 1 November, and bought the stamps for the cards by 1 December? That's the Sensible approach, isn't it?

SENSIBLE SUSAN: Please stop waving that foul cigarette under my nose. And why are you wearing those stupid shoes, Stupid? You know they'll cripple you, why don't you wear sensible shoes like me?

STUPID SUSAN [*laughing heartlessly*]: Because, Sensible, your sensible shoes look like Cornish pasties with straps.

SENSIBLE SUSAN [*shouting*]: At least I'll be able to walk unaided when I'm sixty. You'll be leaning on a Zimmer frame.

STUPID SUSAN [*shouting*]: At least it will be a stylish Zimmer frame. I'll commission one from Zandra Rhodes. It'll have a zebra-skin handle and an inbuilt ashtray and . . .

SENSIBLE SUSAN: You're doing it again! Calm down!

STUPID SUSAN [*sulkily*]: So what do you want for Christmas?

SENSIBLE SUSAN: A grey cardigan that buttons up to the neck, six cotton handkerchiefs and a torch. What do you want?

STUPID SUSAN: I want a pot of chocolate body paint, membership of Madam Jo-Jo's club in Soho and a flagon of Joy perfume.

SENSIBLE SUSAN: You should ask for a bale of towels, Stupid, you haven't got a single matching towel in the house. I know, I've looked.

STUPID SUSAN: You should ask for fishnet stockings. You could always use them to strain the sprouts.

SENSIBLE SUSAN: Can we be sensible now, Stupid? I came round here to ask you about your plans for Christmas. Am I going to you, or you to me?

[*She opens her organizer bag and takes out her electronic organizer. She presses a button and 'Christmas Arrangements' shows on screen.*]

STUPID SUSAN [*pleading*]: You do Christmas this year, Sensible. I forget to post the cards, I leave the giblets in the turkey, my mince pies break people's teeth. Please, I do it every year. It's your turn!

[*But it is too late. Sensible is hurrying towards the travel agent's, where she is hoping to find a late cancellation for a flight to Tobago. She's not stupid.*]

The Discs Cry 'Out!'

I've got sciatica and can't find a comfortable position in which to write. If you've ever had this horrible complaint, you'll know what I mean when I say it brings tears to the eyes and moans to the lips. It also brings 2lb bags of frozen petits pois to the small of the back, but more of that later. I'm now a total back bore, so I'm going to take you, kicking and screaming if necessary, through the story of my bad back.

Susan Townsend, an adventure-playground worker, leaves her healthy outdoor job – building bonfires, constructing tree-houses, dodging stones hurled by maladjusted adolescents – and embarks on a new career. For the next twelve years she spends some of the day and most of the night hunched over a desk, neurotically writing to deadline. Meanwhile, unbeknown to her, inside her body, her spine is protesting. It doesn't like the position it's been forced into. It holds a meeting and after an acrimonious exchange of views between the vertebrae and the discs, the discs leave the meeting, shouting, 'Out! Out! Out!'

Townsend is taken to the chiropractor, where an x-ray

confirms that her lower back should not be shown to medical students as an example of perfection. After manipulation and resting in bed for longer than is tolerable, her spine allows her to get up and continue her hunched position in life. Townsend crams her back into economy-sized seats on long-haul flights, bends double over train tables revising work, takes no exercise apart from the short walk from the house to the taxi. Meanwhile, Townsend starts a new book . . .

The book is called *A Man Walking His Dog*; it is a bleak tale, concerned with death and loss. There is not a laugh in it. Townsend's spine begins to grumble. It protests whenever she rises from a chair, gets out of a car or leans over to empty an ashtray. Townsend writes and rewrites, tears up pages, fights the urge to slip in a few jokes. Deadlines for the book come and go. The publishers, Methuen, are sold to Random House. Townsend's spine is complaining loudly now. Townsend has decided that she cannot work at a desk; she must write at café and restaurant tables, preferably in the open air. She decides this in February, in England. Her spine is now not only hunched, it is also cold. It protests loudly again, so she takes it to Barbados, and it relents and allows her to work.

The book is no longer called *A Man Walking His Dog*. It had a brief life as *A Little Death*, but eventually, after the publishers argue that death is too negative (and who can argue with that?), the title is changed to *Ghost Children*. Eventually, after a frantic period of rewriting and the deleting of thousands and thousands of words (it takes a long time to write a short book) *Ghost Children* is finished. Townsend's spine is surprisingly quiet. She goes to Skyros in Greece to teach writing at the Skyros Centre, and ends up being carried through the main village street by one of her student writers (Alan Clark, handsome and talented). She is semi-delirious; she is laid out on three chairs in Maria's taverna and three doctors, one for each chair, are called for.

One doctor diagnoses lumbago, one diagnoses a kidney infection, one says nothing. She is taken to a hotel next to the island's clinic, and put to bed and nursed by Emma, an indomitable New Zealander.

After a week she returns to England, weak and feeble, her lower vertebrae are whining. There was to be a month set aside to do the house up. Skips were going to be called for to take away the rubbish and junk collected by Townsend over the years. Charity bags were to be filled with her hideous shopping mistakes. Decorators were to be engaged to paint the nicotine-stained walls. Ikea was to be raided. However, it was not to be.

Townsend spends most of the month lounging about feeling not quite right. She books a holiday in Portugal: a villa for two with a swimming pool and hire car, situated along a potholed track (shared by Sir Cliff Richard – the track, that is, not the villa). Anyway, that track was the last straw for the spine, and after another meeting the discs said, 'Out! Out! Out!' We went to the beach twice in fourteen days.

The sciatic nerve is inflamed. Townsend takes to her bed. The pain is vile. Townsend is not brave; she cries out and curses. She is a failure as an invalid. The newspapers would not be able to call her 'brave'. Her husband, who is an honest man, could never say, 'She never complained'. Because I have – especially when the bag of petits pois is clamped to my back every bloody twenty minutes in the hour . . .

Daytime TV

I'm still here, nursing my back. The only time I leave the house is to see somebody with a medical qualification or to have my body bombarded with magnetic particles in a machine that looks like something from the *Star Trek* set. Thank God for books. My reading matter varies wildly, from Martin Amis's new novel *Night Train* (buy it), to booklets from the National Back Pain Association (riveting).

My various engagements and journeys have been cancelled. 'Albania? In February?' The doctor smiled and shook his head and I saw a tragic scenario through his eyes. Townsend, in sciatic agony, is lying in a no-star Albanian hotel room watching the snow blow through a cracked window, crying out for a junior aspirin. People, including my family, find it difficult to believe, but I was looking forward to writing about Albania, and I chose to go in February because winter is when human resources are stretched to the very limit. I was going at the invitation of a new charity, Write Aid, which is the writers' equivalent of Comic Relief, though the only red noses in Albania would have been caused by the cold, I imagine.

However, I do not intend to write myself off and settle into retirement mode. Days before my discs decided to pop out for a stroll along my spine, I bought a pair of purple velvet, peep-toed, slingback platform shoes, and I intend to wear them again, even if it is in the privacy of my own home. In fact, thinking about it dispassionately, I must have looked like mutton dressed as breast of lamb – a very cheap cut – in those shoes.

A thought occurs to me. Did the platform shoes cause the discs to take a stroll? Is my shoe vanity responsible for my present condition? I confess that on two occasions I fell off the platforms. Once in public, at St Pancras station, and once in the changing room in the shop. So is this nature's way of telling me to buy K shoes in future? Could be.

I haven't been in a shop for nine weeks. Nine weeks! Nine weeks without the shopping drug. Talk about cold turkey. One moment I have a clutch of credit cards and the London shops are within pillaging distance, the next I am flat on my back and can't even turn the pages of an Ikea catalogue. Still, like other addicts, I take it one day at a time. It's too early to say that my shopaholism is cured; I won't know that until I face the ultimate test, the K2 of retailing: Bond Street.

In the early days of my incapacitation, when even holding a book or magazine was painful, I watched a lot of daytime television. I grew very fond of Richard and Judy, who seem to me to be proper human beings. However, too many other shows appear to rely on the ritual humiliation of members of the public, whether it be running around a mock supermarket in a frenzy of greed or being shouted at by a professional chef because you can't cook to his standard.

Incidentally, where did professional cooks get the idea

that they should also be stand-up comedians? Would they like it if Jack Dee came on stage and chopped a cabbage? I think not. Most TV cooks are very unfunny indeed, and get their cheap laughs from a gullible studio audience who are so grateful for the free tickets that they would laugh at the death of Little Nell.

There is humiliation overload in the late afternoon on TV, when vastly obese Americans with tragic hairstyles scream, sob and debase themselves in public. 'I slept with the vicar on the eve of my wedding,' confesses one wife. As her husband reels in shock, out from behind the set steps the vicar, a homely, middle-aged woman. As the audience whoops and hollers, the vicar and the wife embrace, and the presenter, svelte in a fitted suit, says, 'Okay, you guys, we have thirty-five seconds to sort this out.' After a few weeks I stopped watching (I wouldn't have bought a ticket for the Colosseum in Rome, either, to watch the Christians being eaten by lions). Call me old-fashioned, but it makes me unhappy to see my fellow humans lose their dignity. That's why, as I hobble to the loo with my walking stick and pass the mirror, I close my eyes tight.

Carpenters on the Run

I've always had a soft spot for carpenters: I idolized Jesus as a child. I used to imagine him and his stepfather Joseph toiling over a lathe, doing things with bits of wood, while Mary stood by, brewing something Middle Eastern in a kettle.

During my secret writing period of twenty years I wrote hundreds of short stories. Many of them concerned woodwork teachers befriending illiterate yobbish schoolboys whose only talent was carpentry. The yob (always called Pete) turned out to be a whiz with wood: producing an exquisite, hand-carved cradle for his girlfriend's illegitimate baby. The cradle was on display at parents' evening, and all who saw it marvelled. The headmaster stroked the carving and, with tears in his eyes, said, 'I've misjudged Pete . . .'

Recently, as part of my master plan to simplify my life, I decided to employ a carpenter/cabinet-maker/joiner. I wanted him to lay floorboards in the attic so that I could stop falling through the joists and store all the junk that I couldn't bear to throw away. I also wanted him to build some bookshelves and storage units in the sitting room.

Please note that my requirements were very simple. I did not ask for the floorboards to be made of a rare walnut only to be found in an inaccessible part of the Amazon jungle, and the shelves and display units did not need an elaborate, Palace of Versailles decorative finish.

But, one by one, three carpenters came, looked at the job, sized it up, then three carpenters left, never to return. Why? This lack of interest brought back all my old insecurities. Did I look like a bad payer? Did the carpenters think they would have to take me to the small claims court before they got paid? Or was it my manner? Did I give them the impression that I would be a difficult temporary employer, standing over them while they laboured, criticizing their workmanship?

Or did the fault lie with the cup of tea I gave them? My sister Barbara once served me a cup of strange-tasting tea. I sipped it politely, then, on finishing it, found half a raw onion which, during cooking, she'd absent-mindedly placed in the cup. Had the carpenters been drinking out of mugs that contained old cloves of garlic, or even drawing pins? It's entirely possible, I'm afraid. Mugs do make handy containers.

Had a grandchild put the chisellers off? Children are capable of saying devastatingly honest things to people (before we teach them to lie). Only last week I heard my two-year-old granddaughter say to the milkman, as she happily handed him the cheque I'd just written, 'Here you are, bald man.' Had the same child made similar vocal observations to the carpenters while I was out of the room? Had they gone off in a huff?

Perhaps there were too many people living in the house, and too many visitors. They may have received the impression that it was some type of institution: a weird religious order or something of the kind.

Something happened to put them off. They were keen enough on the telephone. Is there something in the attic that I don't know about? It's years since I was up there. Is there a bad smell? A decomposing rodent? Has a squirrel broken in and vandalized the place? Is there a wasps' nest hanging in the eaves? Has one of my family got a sinister hobby? Is there evidence of black magic practices up there between the joists? And, if so, why did none of the carpenters say so? They all looked reasonably calm when they climbed back down the loft ladder. One even smiled.

Did they bolt because I was barefoot and wearing pyjamas during the day? If they'd stayed long enough I'd have explained that I was recovering from an operation on my back, and pyjamas are more comfortable, as are bare feet. Could they have scarpered because this is a smoking household? Were they all fanatical non-smokers, afraid of polluting their lungs (though, God knows, I'm sure inhaling sawdust all day can't be good for you)?

They don't know what they're missing. They would have had a good time working in this house: tea, biscuits, cake; a non-judgemental attitude towards lax timekeeping; money upfront for materials; conversation, if they wanted it; parking space for their van . . . As I've said before, it's a mystery. Though one thought does occur. Perhaps, on looking around the house, they may have noticed signs here and there of what I do for a living. Is this what put them all off ? Did they think to themselves: no way am I going to end up as *material* for one of her articles? If this is what happened, let me reassure the carpenters: I wouldn't do such a thing. Please come back. Trust me, I'm a writer.

Cable TV

I do not wish to dwell on my present physical semi-incapacity. My upper lip is as stiff as the next British person's, but I am still inconvenienced enough by my crumbling discs to spend quite a large part of my day in a recumbent position. My clothes from a previous life, the stars of which are a DKNY pinstripe suit, an Agnès B pinstripe suit, and a Ronit Zilkha pinstripe suit, hang unworn on the clothes rail. I no longer have a wardrobe in my bedroom, I moved it out (not personally, it takes me all my time to move the soap in the bath). I kept getting a recurring morbid image of the huge Scandinavian edifice of a wardrobe toppling on to my prone figure and squashing me flat.

I'm no longer a woman who wears pinstripe suits and high heels. I slouch through the day in the equivalent of grown-up toddler wear – everything is fleecy and elasticated, and can be washed at 40°C and tumble-dried. I only wear shoes on my twice-weekly visits to see Nita, my physiotherapist, and the shoes are flat and hideous – the type that religious fundamentalists and chiropodists approve of. The rest of the time, in the house, I wear bootee-like mountaineering socks. My hairstyle is also toddler-like, having been scraped up into a scrunchie so that I have a hank of hair sticking up on the top of my head. All in all, I look like a middle-aged Teletubby, though sadly without their charm and innocent exuberance.

I spend my days waving my arms and legs about, performing Nita's exercises and also sitting on my heightened lavatory (borrowed from the Red Cross), complete with guardrails – more infantilization.

A few weeks ago, in one of those pathetic attempts to keep up-to-date, we had cable television installed. A ludicrous decision, considering we only ever watch Channel Four, out of the five terrestrial stations. A little man turned up to connect us. Please don't think I am patronizing the labouring classes. He was a very little man. Four feet eight inches in big boots would be a generous estimate of his stature. He looked a little alarmed when he saw me, the householder, lurching towards him in my Teletubby gear. But he recovered and went into a long spiel about how he would have to knock a hole in the garden wall, uproot trees and disfigure the front of the house, in order to fit the cable into a bedroom and a sitting room. He was like the Ancient Mariner, projecting doom and gloom. 'But,' I stuttered, 'the salesman . . .'

'Salesman!' he repeated, contemptuously. He practically spat the word out. It appears that a Grand Canyon-like chasm exists between the silver-tongued sellers and the pragmatic installers. As the customer's hand is guided towards the contract, no mention is made of holes in walls or the felling of trees or the despoiling of lawns. Of course the customer should have asked about these practicalities, but the poor sap has been bedazzled by Mr Silver Tongue, who is on commission, and has used all of his wily skills to convince the householders that their dull lives will be magically enhanced by being able to watch forty-eight television channels.

The little man stood and waited impatiently in the hallway while I agonized over which shrub in the garden I should sacrifice. Eventually, I pointed to the chosen one. A 'Bridal Bouquet' shrub which had looked less like a bridal bouquet and more like a widow's weeds last spring. The little man and his companion set to work and, six cups of tea later, cable was installed. It was an immaculate job. These men should be employed by Military Intelligence. There was no sign that they had ever been anywhere near my house. I can only speculate that the little man's initial doom-laden speech was a type of verbal insurance policy, should any damage occur.

Three weeks later and what do we watch, now that the world of television is at our fingertips? Channel Four. For a week I watched QVC, the shopping channel. It was quite amusing in a hideous kind of way to watch the salespeople / presenters almost come to orgasm as they demonstrated the virtues of a can of oven cleaner or a deep-fat fryer. In thirty-six hours of watching I didn't see anything I wanted or needed. When mocked by family and friends during my shopping-channel marathon, I told them that I was thinking of 'writing something about popular culture'. But secretly I was longing for something desirable to come on – books or elasticated large-sized toddler wear or even, dare I say it, a decent pinstripe women's suit.

The Silver Boob Tube

I'm fifty-two years old this month, not young, not old. I'm still wearing my leather jacket, which, unlike me, is ageing beautifully. However, I've worn my last pair of denim jeans and I certainly won't replace the hoop earrings that I now realize make me look as if I tell fortunes in an end-of-the-pier booth. I know I've written about clothes before in this column, but one of my obsessions is clothes, and the messages they convey to others.

I keep coming across a perfectly nice woman who works in a factory, although she dresses in the style of a cartoon prostitute – more trash than trailer. She is in her early thirties, and is the mother of a school-age boy. I overheard her once, complaining to her conservatively dressed mother that the foreman at work had asked her to dress 'more respectably'. She was obviously hurt, offended and surprised.

'What's up wi' 'ow I dress?' she asked her grey-haired, slipper-clad mum. Her massive cleavage almost wobbled out of its silver boob tube as she defended her right to wear what she pleased to work. She is obviously a frustrated performer. The woman was born to fly through the tense air of a circus tent on a trapeze. Sitting behind a factory bench is a complete waste of her splendid, fishnetted thighs.

Her husband doesn't care for her exhibitionistic style either; he's been asking her to 'tone it down' lately. She thinks he's jealous because other men stare at her. Other men certainly do stare at her, as do women and children; even dogs must have given her the odd backward glance.

I have never been introduced to this woman, and she doesn't know me. I am only conversant with her life and her grievances because she possesses an incredibly loud voice (older readers think Gracie Fields, younger readers, Scary Spice). She conducts conversations as though she is standing on the cliffs at Dover, and the person she is talking to is on the harbour at Calais. She would make an excellent town crier, though she'd soon have the hem of the robe turned up and the neckline slashed. I hope for the sake of her neighbours she lives in a detached house. It doesn't bear thinking about, what you'd hear through her party wall.

She is very fond of 1950s rock and roll, which she plays extremely loudly on her car stereo. You can hear her approaching when she's still several streets away. Her car doesn't simply pull up at the kerb, it screeches to an emergency stop. Other, weaker women might sustain whiplash injuries from the constant stress on the neck, but you're not likely to see her in a surgical collar and if you did, she'd have customized it with sequins and a bit of cowboy fringing.

She is an example, I suppose, of what D. H. Lawrence called 'life force'. She is a living, breathing piece of unselfconscious performance art. As she goes about her day, she must amuse and enrage hundreds of people. She is almost certainly the subject of endless anecdotes. From what I've heard, she is engaged in a constant battle with authority.

She knows her rights and makes sure she gets them. She would make a splendid MP (Independent). I can see that it would be highly embarrassing at times to have a mother like her. The thought of her attending parents' evening at her son's school brings a blush to my cheek. Which is ridiculous because, as I've already said, I don't even know the woman, not even her name.

I hope she's called something suitable to her looks and personality: Lola, for instance. I couldn't bear it if she were called Joan Smith.

There used to be many such individualistic characters around when I was a child. There was the man in a leopard-skin leotard, who wrapped himself in chains outside the entrance of a department store. He would only struggle free when enough money had been thrown into his top hat. Local rumour had it that he was a millionaire, but I saw him towards the end of his escapologist career, standing at a bus stop with his chains in a shopping bag, so I don't think he had untold riches.

There was Cyril the gay barman, who wore high heels behind the bar of the toughest pub in town. All the yobs lived in fear of his cruel tongue. Sarcasm doesn't kill, but it can leave deep wounds.

We're all so much more conservative now, even punks look like establishment figures. So I take my boring black hat off to the woman with the loud voice and the loud clothes. May your sequins never tarnish, may your fishnets never snag and may you grow old very disgracefully indeed.

Information Overload

Only last week I was complaining to my husband about the ridiculous number of newspapers and magazines that are delivered to us. Every morning there is a thick wad of them lying on the hall floor. All that news, all that information, all that opinion. Page after page to be ploughed through. There's hardly time left in the day to wash, dress and feed myself, let alone do any work.

The weekend is entirely given over to newspaper reading. Other people go shopping, do the gardening or socialize, but I've got over forty separate supplements, colour or otherwise, to get through before Monday morning brings another fresh crop of broadsheets. Meanwhile, the weekly, fortnightly and monthly magazines are piling up, unread, on surfaces all over the house. When I enter a room they shriek, 'Read me! Read me!' Well, perhaps they don't, but it feels like that.

So, last week, I announced that I was cancelling the papers, not for a fortnight while we went on holiday, but for ever. I was suffering from information overload, I said, and my brain could take no more. This reached crisis point yesterday when I found myself watching a test match on TV, while simultaneously listening to the Radio 4 commentary and reading the *Daily Telegraph*'s cricketing correspondent. And I still don't understand the damn leg before wicket rules.

'If a big news story breaks, I'll walk to the newsagent's and buy a newspaper over the counter,' I said to my husband, who probably wasn't listening, but nodded his head anyway. Every time I passed the overflowing recycling bins (note the plural), I meant to telephone and break the bad news to the newsagent, but somehow I failed to do this.

I kept imagining his face as he drew a thick black line through our mega-order in his accounts book. Surely this cancellation would represent a serious drop in his family's income? Would he have to take a child out of private nursery school? Would it mean a downward spiral into debt and eventual bankruptcy? Would he turn to drink, end up divorced and only be given access to his children on alternate Sundays?

It's OK, I've just got up and walked around the room. I'm calmer now. My rational self knows that the cancellation of our papers will not lead to our newsagent's premature death from liver disease. But even so . . .

This morning, my husband announced that he'd had an exciting letter from a woman called Dorothy Addeo. I snatched it out of his hand. She had written: 'The fact is, Mr Broadway, your home in Leicester has been identified as a possible location for an Extraordinary Future Event.'

I speculated as to what this extraordinary event could be. A millennium celebration, perhaps? Dorothy's letter continued: 'It's morning, Mr Broadway. You're at home getting ready to start the day. Deciding what to have for breakfast, perhaps, or what to wear for work. Suddenly a commotion in the street draws you to the window. You see a security van pull up outside. Out steps a distinguished, silver-haired gentleman with a locked box handcuffed to his wrist. Flanked on each side by guards, he strides purposefully to your door.

'The doorbell rings. When you open the door, Dave Sayer of the Publishers' Clearing House Prize Patrol greets you with, "Mr Broadway, you're our newest multimillionaire. And I've brought all your millions." With that, he unlocks the box and reveals £2,200,000 in cash, right there before your eyes! I'll bet you never thought you'd live to see that much money all at once – in cash!'

You can tell by the proliferating exclamation marks that Dorothy is getting excited, and perhaps it's as well that Dave Sayer takes over. He writes to my husband: 'Dear Winner Candidate. If you are our £2,200,000 winner, we'd soon be at your door, along with a TV news crew, to record the winning moment for the entire country to see. As a friend and potential millionaire, you understand that the only way we can afford to give away so much money is to sell magazines . . .'

At this point I stopped reading Dave's letter and glanced at a sheet of perforated, stamp-sized magazine covers, helpfully supplied by Dorothy. Among the likes of *Choir and Organ*, *Koi Carp* and *Muscle and Fitness*, I found a stamp for *London Review of Books*. I tore it off and stuck it on the prizewinners' acceptance coupon. From now on I shall keep watch at my window every morning, eagerly awaiting a commotion in the street.

Full-nest Syndrome

They're gone. I wander in and out of empty, echoing rooms. Sometimes I take a chair with me, sit in the space and listen to the silence.

We have four grown-up children, ranging in age from twenty-one to thirty-two. Their various leave-takings have been spread over ten years, but the pattern has been that, as soon as we closed the door on one child, another would open it, asking for sanctuary. They were refugees from ill-fated love affairs or financial crises, or both (in fact, usually both). No reasonable parent can refuse their children shelter from the storm, though it's true that they often bring bad weather with them: clouds of depression and fogs of misunderstanding can settle over the house.

The sun shines very rarely when there's a grown-up child skulking upstairs, recovering from a broken heart. You can't exactly sit him on your knee and promise that, if he's a good boy, you'll let him put the jam in the jam tarts. Neither can you order him to shave, wash his horrible hair or go to bed at a reasonable time. His broken heart will not heal any faster by loose talk about Fishes In The Sea – and since we're on the subject of advice, never, ever criticize the heart-breaker. I once cracked (under great provocation, m'lud), and shouted, 'I hope she falls under a lorry!' Uncharitable, I know, and also very stupid, as the heartbroken and the heartbreaker were passionately reunited within a week and he moved out, leaving six cereal bowls under the bed and the lingering smell of misery, which defies all air fresheners.

Other people have pointed out that the lingering smell of misery is a laughable, pretentious idea, and that the most likely cause of the pong in the vacated room is that a small rodent has died and is decomposing beneath the floorboards. I prefer my misery theory: the thought of pulling up all those floorboards . . .

People ask me, 'What's it like now the kids have gone?' I reply, 'It's like being on holiday.' Though to be more accurate, it's like being on honeymoon. We can smooch on the sofa as much as we like now without springing apart guiltily at the sound of a grown-up child's footsteps outside the door.

Other women suffer from empty-nest syndrome and turn towards car maintenance classes or amateur dramatic societies to fill the void in their lives. I now realize that it was the opposite with me. I suffered badly from full-nest syndrome. I found the responsibilities of being a parent overwhelming at times.

I was a tense mother. My first child was premature and lived in an incubator for the first month of his life. He was cared for round the clock by highly trained doctors and nurses, whereas I was an untrained, daft-as-a-brush nineteen-year-old. The closest I'd been to a baby was looking at the illustrations in Doctor Spock's *The Common Sense Book of Baby and Child Care*.

Incidentally, I have never understood why poor Doctor Spock was, and still is, so vilified. Only the other day I heard one of his detractors on the radio blaming Spock's liberalism for today's hooligans, litter louts and vandals.

My memories of Spock's writings are quite different. I will never forget his stern advice on how to stop a toddler getting out of its cot several times a night. He counselled the child's sleep-deprived parents to throw a badminton net over the cot, tie it securely at each corner and to close their ears to the child's screams. Such harsh pragmatism could have come straight from the Ann Widdecombe Book of Kiddie Care.

When the baby came out of hospital he weighed only five pounds. It was handy that he was so small, because he had to be smuggled in and out of the flat. The landlord didn't allow babies to live on his property. When not going in or out of the front door with the baby secreted inside my coat, I was crouched over the carrycot, taking his pulse and checking that he hadn't stopped breathing. I now know that this is normal behaviour for most parents (the checking, not the smuggling), but then, at nineteen, I was convinced that I'd fail to keep this fragile kid alive. Each morning I would approach his cot with dread, then I'd see his eyes open, or an arm wave, and I'd consider it a miracle and I'd feel, temporarily, like a proper mother.

Somehow I managed to keep him and three others alive. Today they're hale and occasionally hearty, and they each have their own postcode. More importantly, they now have other people who love and care for them. Perhaps now I can safely put that badminton net away.

Gipton Estate

'**It used to** be a lovely place to live twenty years ago.' I heard this from older people everywhere I went on the Gipton Council Estate in Leeds. And, if you squinted and used your imagination, you could see that once upon a time the Gipton would have been a pleasant place to bring up a family – the streets are wide, there is open space where children can play, and the houses are spacious. However, once you open your eyes, you cannot help but notice that the estate has suffered a terrible calamity.

There is a type of bomb stored in the arsenals of the superpowers that kills people but does not destroy buildings. The opposite has happened here. The infrastructure is dead, but the people have survived and are picking their way through the ruins.

I was there some time ago, but I am still haunted by what I saw. I cannot get the pictures of the burnt-out houses, the wrecked pavements and the boarded-up shops to leave my mind. It is difficult to believe that this can be a location in England, or to comprehend that Leeds City Centre, shining with hi-tech prosperity, is only a 70 pence bus fare away.

Outsiders described the Gipton residents as 'animals'. This word was used so often that I wouldn't have been surprised to see giraffes and elephants grazing in the overgrown gardens of the abandoned houses. Describing people as animals dehumanizes them; it strips away their dignity and suggests that they have no feelings; that if they are hurt they feel no pain; that if they are poor they deserve to suffer, to be poverty stricken.

The people on the Gipton Estate are, of course, part of common humanity. In my time there, I was never spoken to unkindly, and at no time did I feel in danger, though I had heard terrible stories from people afraid to leave their homes for fear of burglary or arson.

The young are desperate for money for drugs, in particular crack cocaine, and the old criminal code, that you do not steal from your own kind, has long been breached by them. The dictatorship of the male teenager prevails on the Gipton, as it does in so many estates, inner cities and villages. Future generations will look back at our social records and be curious as to how such a small group of poor, powerless boys could have had such a terrible effect on so many communities.

When I was a teenager I didn't know a youth or a man who didn't have a job, and it was the same on the Gipton. The young men got up in the morning and went to work. Twenty years ago, there would be a conductor on the bus to keep an eye on the top deck. There would be a park keeper to watch over the new saplings. There would be enough caretakers to keep the public buildings clean. The council employed sufficient workmen to maintain properties before they became an eyesore. Local shops thrived because people had wages to spend; the pubs and social clubs were where you met your neighbours. The work was often very hard, but there were certainly compensations: people went on factory outings and dressed up for the annual dinner dance. And, most importantly, the older men and women were not afraid to be adults; they watched over the young and kept them in check.

Then the work went, and the local authority cuts meant that there was less money for repairs. The bus conductors went. The park keeper was given a moped and a larger territory to patrol. Caretakers struggled with fewer staff and could no longer care. Meanwhile, on the television, night after night, the newly poor were exhorted to buy things they could no longer afford. Is it any wonder they began to feel alienated from the mainstream of society? Before they knew it, these people who had lost their work were being called the 'underclass'.

It is almost impossible to talk or write about poverty without sounding like the greatly missed Les Dawson, but I did have to keep children away from school because they had no shoes to wear. And I knew exactly, down to the last sultana, what was in my food cupboard. A school trip, a lost purse, a child's birthday, would play havoc with the tightest financial restraint. Disaster was always round the corner.

Freud is reputed to have said, 'To be happy a person needs two things: love and work.'

People can find love for themselves, but work needs to be found for them, as a matter of the greatest urgency.

Conservatories

My gardening obsession has taken a turn for the worse. This weekend, a room in the house was demolished to give me more growing space. Calling it a room is perhaps an exaggeration, but it certainly had a floor, a door and windows and, in summer, was home to several hundred bees, hence its nickname – The Bee House. Quite an evocative title considering that this room was a glorified lean-to.

Occasionally a visitor would remark (inaccurately), 'Oh, you have a conservatory,' and you could almost see the wretched lean-to take on airs and graces and start fancying itself, and thinking that it deserved to be adorned with exotic palms and orchids instead of the boxes of washing powder, odd socks and dead bees of its mundane, everyday life.

I was once interviewed by a journalist whose husband was the Mr Big of the conservatory world. She explained that it was a well-known fact that couples who wanted a conservatory inevitably had problems with their marriage, and that just as some married fools think that another baby will heal their festering relationship (ha!), others think a glass room with wicker furniture and plants will do the trick.

Incidentally, the interview was abandoned halfway through. She took a phone call during which her hand went to her throat, the colour drained from her face and she said to me, 'You'll have to leave, right now.' I ran from the house and she passed me, running, on the pavement. For a few days I speculated on the reason for our hasty departures. A bomb threat from a disaffected conservatory owner? A lover threatening to jump from the top of Canary Wharf? A child forgotten at the school gates?

To get back to conservatories. Why are they so desirable? A straw poll reveals that people want conservatories because:

a they will gain space
b they will be able to see more of the garden
c they will be able to grow exotic plants and fruits, such as peaches and nectarines
d (women only) they will be able to lie on a wicker sofa and read a book at the weekend
e (men only) it will be somewhere dry where they can work on that old car engine in peace at the weekend

Whereas a straw poll of conservatory owners reveals:

a no space is gained; a conservatory becomes a repository for household junk
b you cannot see the garden or the sky or the tops of the trees because of the sun blinds you have been forced to fit

c you cannot grow exotic plants, due to excessive drying out during your absence on holiday. Teenage children are congenitally unable to water any living thing (cannabis is probably the only exception)

d you will be uncomfortably hot in the summer, unpleasantly cold in the winter, and anyway, you will be driven mad by the creaking of the wicker every time you turn a page of that book

e no, there are no miracle products on the market at the moment that will remove engine oil stains from terracotta tiles, pvc windows or wicker

So the room / lean-to / Bee House and almost-conservatory is gone. A husband, a son and a son-in-law wrestled the thing down on Saturday. On Sunday we gathered on what was left of it – the floor – and people started to call it 'the terrace'. I've always thought of a terrace as a place where aristocrats go to be sick after drinking too much at a ball, so another name will have to be found for it.

I must watch this lust for horticulture, though. Last weekend I found myself in a queue at the garden centre checkout, sneering openly at an old bloke's trolley that was filled with red salvia. Earlier, I had eavesdropped on a conversation between two middle-aged women who were bent over an azalea.

First Woman: 'What's that?' Second Woman (reading label): 'It's an azalea.' FW: 'No, it can't be. I bought an azalea last week and it was nothing like that; it had different leaves and different-coloured flowers.' SW: 'It's got the wrong label on, then. I wonder what it is?'

I stopped myself from lecturing them about the hundreds of varieties of azaleas available, but it was a near thing. I had to remind myself that my own ignorance about computers, driving a car or the situation in the Middle East is equally profound.

Scientific Studies
Are Silly

I have been sceptical about scientific reports ever since I read that Australian scientists had found that apples were bad for children's teeth. Being as I had spent years forcing Granny Smiths and Discoveries down my children's throats in the belief that an apple a day would keep them from harm of all kinds – vitamin deficiency, constipation and, yes, dental caries – I think I was entitled to feel more than a little disgruntled with the boffins.

A few years ago I was told that I was in urgent need of vitamin B6; I now read that B6 is as dodgy as an Arthur Daley cutlery set, and about as good for you if swallowed. Where are we now in regard to the efficacy of margarine? I've lost track. Is it good for you or not? Does it clog the arteries or doesn't it? Is eating a lightly boiled egg as risky as abseiling from the top of the Empire State Building? Is British beef safe to eat, or is ingesting a T-bone steak an act of foolhardy recklessness equivalent to throwing yourself over Niagara Falls in a leaking barrel?

A long scientific study has reported that dolphins are highly intelligent creatures that, if given the chance, would spend their time reading *The London Review of Books*, listening to Wagner and discussing the Turner Prize on *Late Night Line Up*. Again, I don't trust the white coats on this one. As far as I know, the height of dolphinkind's achievements are in a dolphinarium, where they are applauded for jumping out of a pool to snatch a fish from the hand of a blonde in a wetsuit. And if they're so clever, how come they keep getting caught in those Japanese nets? Why don't they swim the other way? Have they got highly developed communication skills or haven't they?

But the latest report I read has drained my sceptic storage tank dry. It said, 'Scientists have discovered that giraffes, previously thought to be dumb, can communicate. Some use regional accents.'

I am a great admirer of giraffes. My first glimpse of male genitalia came courtesy of Barry, a stuffed giraffe that stood at the top of a flight of mahogany stairs in a Leicester museum. Barry was a hard act to follow. Generations of Leicester men have been traumatized by Barry's generous endowments and it put quite a few Leicester women off men, I can tell you.

I do not like zoos of any kind. They are prisons for animals, heartbreak hotels for the furred and feathered. However, I have captives of my own: four goldfish that live a life of indolent luxury. They spend their days in a huge hexagonal tank with Japanese-influenced interior decoration. They enjoy gravel, a bamboo art work and an artfully placed log. Their water is filtered and they are beautifully lit from above by a fetching violet light. They are fed on the finest fish flakes, but do they look happy? No, they do not. They look reproachfully at me through the walls of the tank. I can't decide if they are pining for the freedom of the China Sea or just gormlessly waiting for more fish flakes.

Lobster is definitely off my menu after reading an extract from *The Shellfish Network Newsletter*. Dr Loren G. Horsely, invertebrate zoologist, informs shellfish aficionados that:

Lobsters have a sophisticated nervous system, and feel pain when cut or cooked
Lobsters carry their young for nine months and have a long childhood and awkward adolescence
Some lobsters are right-handed, and some are left
They have been seen walking hand in hand, the old leading the young

I do hope that a huddle of white coats are not studying others in the crustacean family. I do not want to know that:

Prawns celebrate birthdays
Prawns go through a kind of marriage service
Prawns sing to their young
Crabs very much enjoy formation dancing
Crabs die of a broken heart if their spouse commits adultery

I hate the anthropomorphism of animals. Why do we feel the need to project our own human vileness on to the savage creatures we share the world with? I asked a few giraffes of my acquaintance for their opinions on human beings.

Mr Neck of Twycross said, 'Well m'duck, humans are nowt but trouble, they're either chuckin' doughnuts at you or staring at your private parts.'

Mr Longlegs of Windsor Safari Park drawled, 'Actually,

one is frightfully amused by the humans that come to gawk at one through the steamed-up windows of their horrid little cars.'

Ms G. McRaff of Glasgow Zoo paused from tearing leaves from a tall tree to say, 'Och! I dinna gi' a toss about humans, it's just scientists I canna' stand.'

Christmas Insurance

Sir Andrew Murdstone sat behind the large grey metal desk in his office on the twentieth floor of Murdstone Towers. It was Christmas Eve.

Murdstone Insurance Ltd (slogan: 'You Are Safe in Our Hands') was the most successful insurance company in the land. Money poured in; by direct debit, by standing order, and even (quaintly) from old-fashioned insurance men who collected cash on a weekly basis.

Sir Andrew didn't like Christmas. The public became careless. They drank too much, and stayed up too late, and walked around in a fog of exhaustion. They lost their keys and their overcoats; they left their handbags on the bus. Their shopping bags, full of Christmas presents, were thrown on to the back seat of their cars, where they were stolen by wicked boys who could not believe their luck.

Christmas was a bad time for the insurance industry. It brought with it bizarre accidents. Sir Andrew shuddered as he recalled the statistics.

Eleven thousand people had submitted claims after suffering lacerations to their fingers from sticky-tape dispensers while wrapping presents. Fifteen thousand dogs had destroyed their owners' Christmas trees.

Three (separate) rabbits had chewed through fairy-light flexes causing, in each case, small electrical fires. Ten thousand women had slipped on turkey fat and broken their legs. Five women had attacked their husbands with carving knives after being criticized because the roast potatoes were 'not crispy enough'. Two of these women subsequently received prison sentences.

Sir Andrew was disturbed by these statistics. He drummed his fingers on top of his metal desk. It made an unpleasant, tinny sound. For a moment, he regretted throwing out his oak desk, then he remembered the figures for infected fingers caused by splinters of wood, and knew he'd done the right thing. He lived by the maxim, 'minimize the risk'.

He carried this philosophy into every aspect of his life: he had married a sensible woman called Ann. They had met at a badminton club, and had played regularly until Andrew (he was not Sir Andrew then) discovered that eye injuries, caused by shuttlecocks, were increasing by 12 per cent a year.

He had decided not to have children. He had said to his wife, 'Children cause chaos in the home, Ann.' She had looked a little pensive at the time, but she had soon recovered. Sir Andrew went to the panoramic window and looked down at the gridlocked traffic below. He noticed that several cars had Christmas trees lashed to the roof racks. He hoped they were not insured with Murdstone Insurance. He had been forced to pay out £300,000 in claims due to Christmas trees falling into the path of moving traffic.

His secretary, Marcia, came into the office. He noticed she was wearing extremely high red platform shoes.

He pointed to her feet and said, 'Marcia, do you know how many women break their ankles every year in those things?'

Marcia said, rather defiantly he thought, 'Yes, Sir Andrew, last year Murdstone Insurance paid out three-quarters of a million pounds in claims to women who had fallen off their platform shoes.' 'Then why are you wearing them?' he asked. 'They're party shoes,' she said. 'I'm going to have fun in them.' She gave him a present, and wished him happy Christmas as she hobbled out of the office on her dangerous red shoes.

Sir Andrew unwrapped the present at his desk. It was a scented candle in a snowman-decorated tin. He was out-raged. Had Marcia gone mad? Had she learned nothing from her years of working in the insurance industry? Festive candles caused hundreds of thousands of household fires at Christmas. He trembled when he recalled the damage done to the average living room by a high-pressure hose and a team of enthusiastic firemen. He picked up the telephone and called his wife. She took a long time to answer. 'What kept you?' he said.

'I was lighting the logs in the fireplace,' she replied.

His throat constricted; he could hardly speak. The stat-istics for chimney fires flashed in front of his eyes. He truly loved Ann, but he would have to divorce her now. He could not live with a woman who took such risks. He picked up his briefcase and turned out the lights. He slipped on the carelessly discarded Christmas paper. He fell and hit his head against the sharp edge of his metal desk. Before he lapsed into unconsciousness he wrote 'Acts of God' in blood on the side of the desk.

Strangers on a Train

Dublin was basking in the autumn heatwave. Dubliners thronged the streets wearing the clothes they'd only recently packed away. I was far from home and unsuitably dressed in layers of wool.

I felt like a sheep on heat as I dragged my little suitcase on wheels down the platform at Connolly station. I was looking for a quiet seat where I could pass the three-and-a-half-hour journey to Sligo in silence. I was halfway through a publicity tour and the yak, yak, yak of my voice had become repulsive to me.

I found a seat at the front of the train. There was an empty table seat for four opposite me, across the aisle. I prayed it would remain empty. I felt that conversation was beyond me, especially the Irish conversation, for which you need a quick brain and an even quicker tongue. Two minutes before the train was due to depart I congratulated myself that I would be left in peace.

Then there was a commotion on the platform. A young teenager – a boy with a shaven head – ran to the door of the carriage where I was sitting and jerked it open, shouting, 'Here, Ma, there's seats here.'

A fat woman dressed in leggings and a pink T-shirt ran towards the open door. She was carrying a four-year-old girl in her arms. Another, medium-sized girl (seven, perhaps) staggered towards the carriage, handicapped by the kiddie-style high heels she wore. At the rear came a big girl in a track suit.

The train groaned out of the station and I groaned with it. The shouting family burst into the carriage and made for the empty seats across from me.

The carrier bags were stowed in the overhead luggage rack, then they were all dragged down again because Ma wanted her fags and couldn't remember which bag they were in.

Everyone talked at once, each shouting to be heard above the others. I turned away and stared fixedly out of the window.

The book I was publicizing was about abortion and children and good and bad parenting, and I had yacked on numerous radio stations and in many book shops about what constitutes a good parent. What followed was to put my theories to the test.

A quarter of an hour into the journey, Ma told the children to 'Go and play'; she wanted some peace. The children left her side instantly. The seven-year-old stood on tiptoe and stuck her head out of the window. The four-year-old introduced various objects to the nozzle of a fire extinguisher. The boy announced he was going to have a chat with the driver, and the big girl made a banner out of toilet paper, which she waved vigorously out of the train.

Half an hour into the journey, Ma made her way to

the buffet car. She came back with two large bottles of Budweiser, five jumbo-sized Mars bars and five packets of crisps. She bellowed to the children and they rejoined her instantly. She drank from one of the bottles and told the children to share the other. It was quite a sight to see the little one spit her dummy from her mouth, take a swig of beer, smack her lips, then replace the dummy.

When the crisp packets and sweet wrappers had been thrown on to the floor, the big girl said, 'I'm still hungry, Ma.'

Ma handed cash over to the girl, who went to the buffet car and returned with five more jumbo-sized Mars bars. My thin English lips pursed in disapproval as I watched this calorific overindulgence.

At half-hourly intervals, Ma went off to the buffet car and returned with two bottles of beer, one of which she gave to the children, who passed it amongst themselves with scrupulous fairness.

When they were all merry (drunk), Ma asked them to sing to her. And they did. In tune, word perfect, using harmony and hand gestures. The four-year-old took her dummy out, stood on the table and sang 'Tomorrow' from *Annie*.

I was bewitched but also bothered and bewildered. As they stood waiting to get off, I caught Ma's eye. 'Lovely children,' I said. A grim-faced man was waiting for them on the platform. Ma and the children fell slowly silent as they followed his unwelcoming back.

Dr Strudel Questions
Mrs Townsend

I forgot the alphabet the other day. I sat at my desk (ex-kitchen table) and struggled to remember which letter came after G. I started again at A, but stalled again at G. I closed my eyes and concentrated very hard indeed, but G's right-hand neighbour continued to elude me. I then sang the alphabet, something I haven't done since infant school, but the damned letter refused to leave the dark recesses of my brain. Eventually, though, H sidled out with its hands up, saying, 'OK, you've found me, it's a fair cop.'

Should I book myself into a daycare centre soon? I believe that before they let you in they make you sit a sort of test.

The first question they ask is usually, 'Do you know what day it is today?'

Now, I pride myself on being quite sharp and agile-brained about those interesting, dramatic days – Friday, Saturday, Sunday and Monday – but I confess to frequently confusing the more prosaic, dull days in the middle of the week; Tuesday, Wednesday and Thursday lack the energy, the excitement, of the Weekend Four. I can't imagine a bloody revolution being planned for a Wednesday. And whoever staged a coup d'état on a Thursday? As for Tuesday, it's a snivelling, apologetic, whining kind of day. It begs to be forgotten.

So, if I'm questioned in the middle of the week, I may fail the day test.

Another question is: 'Who is the Prime Minister?'

I'm very confident about naming the leader of our nation – it's Peter Mandelson. The Prime Minister is Tony Blair, and another thing I know for sure is that he is married to a smiling woman called Cherie Blair, who seems to have lost the power of speech.

Mrs Blair should not be confused with Ms Cherie Booth, who is an articulate barrister.

Other diagnostic tests for cognitive functioning consist of simple mental arithmetic questions. I would fail these without doubt.

An observer wrote the following:

The questioner, Dr Strudel, asked in a kindly manner: 'Mrs Townsend, what is two plus two plus two?'

Mrs Townsend didn't appear to understand the question. She asked for it to be repeated.

Dr Strudel carefully rephrased the question, asking, 'Mrs Townsend, what is three times two?'

Mrs Townsend repeated the question to herself, her lips moving as she did so. She shook her head and became visibly agitated. Her neck and chest became bathed in perspiration.

Mrs Townsend made several attempts to count up to six, but each time she lost track of how many fingers she had counted, and had to go back to a thumb and start again.

Eventually, Dr Strudel said, with a hint of pity, 'We'll forget the sums, shall we?'

Mrs Townsend wiped her palms and said, 'I can't do sums

under test conditions, but I'm very good at capital cities of South American countries.' Dr Strudel shook his head sadly and continued to ask the questions attached to his clipboard.

DR STRUDEL: How many kettles have you left on the hob in the past month, Mrs Townsend?

MRS TOWNSEND [*angrily*]: Who's been talking?

DR STRUDEL: How many kettles?

MRS TOWNSEND: Four! Is it a crime? None of them burned out!

DR STRUDEL: Do you have an umbrella?

MRS TOWNSEND: No, I think I left it in British Home Stores.

DR STRUDEL: Are you absent-minded?

MRS TOWNSEND: I can't remember. But if you want to know the capital of Guatemala . . .

DR STRUDEL: What's my name, Mrs Townsend?

MRS TOWNSEND: Er, I'm bad on names, but give me a minute. It's something to do with apples . . . Er, Dr Crumble?

DR STRUDEL: No. Not Crumble.

MRS TOWNSEND: Dr Pippin?

DR STRUDEL: No.

MRS TOWNSEND: Dr Cox!

DR STRUDEL: No!

MRS TOWNSEND: Dr Pie? Dr Peel? Dr Braeburn? [*Suddenly standing up*] I've got to go.

The observer writes:

As she ran from the interview room, Mrs Townsend shouted, 'I've got to go home! I've just remembered I've left the kettle on the hob!'

DR STRUDEL [*Shouting*]: I would like you to make another appointment.

The observer writes:

I pointed out to Dr Strudel that Mrs Townsend would have to return as she had forgotten to take her handbag, her coat and her purse.

A nurse later reported having seen a woman without a coat walking in the rain, muttering the names of South American capital cities to herself. This woman is believed to be Mrs Townsend.

Dogs

Dogs have featured in several of my novels. In the Adrian Mole books, the Mole family dog has no name, and no sex – it is simply known as 'The Dog'. The dog is a damned nuisance. It is constantly at the vets' having its stomach x-rayed, it follows Adrian to school, and it is always standing in front of the television.

The Moles have a love / hate relationship with their mongrel, as does Christopher, a character in my latest book, *Ghost Children*. His dog is a bull terrier, and, again, it has no gender and no name. The dogs in these books represent anarchy and chaos, they precipitate events. They are also a convenient story-telling device.

Dogs do things that humans are unable to do (except psychopaths or people reared by wolves). Dogs have no conscience; they do not suffer from feelings of guilt. They do not wake in the night, drenched in sweat, thinking about their latest faux pas. Dogs don't suffer from existential angst.

They certainly don't care what name you've had engraved on their identity disc or collar. Call a toy poodle 'Butcher' and it will happily trot towards you. Shout 'Fifi' to your Dobermann in the park and it will lunge at you with great delight. Dogs don't bear grudges. But I don't have a good track record with dogs, which is why *chez* Townsend has been dogless for twenty years.

The last canine encumbrance was a mad swirl of long hair and nervous energy called Lola. We drove many miles to pick her up from a breeder of bearded collies.

Lola was the last puppy to be sold. She was obviously the runt of the litter. She ran around the breeders' garden in ever-decreasing circles chasing her bush of a tail. She yapped continuously. She had a mad look in her eyes. We bought her.

I still shudder when I think of the journey home.

Over the next few months, several unpleasant characteristics emerged: Lola hated bicycles and would attack them ferociously. She also took a dislike to elderly people, which was particularly unfortunate as we lived opposite an old folks' home at the time. She developed a hatred for upholstered furniture, which she tore apart until it was dead. Lola urinated and defecated wherever she happened to be at the time, although her preference was for a piece of newly laid carpet.

I know what you're thinking: 'I blame the owners,' and you are probably right. Dogs are thick, but they sense when their owners are timid and unconfident. And it has to be said that, twenty years ago, I was that sad creature, and Lola took advantage of me.

She had to go, and she went. The details are murky. My husband put her in the car and came back an hour later without her. When the children asked where she was, he muttered something about a 'farm', 'a kind farmer', 'Lola will be happy'. That sort of thing.

I knew better than to pin him down about it. He had the conscience-stricken look of a murderer about him. It wasn't the first time he'd done my dirty work.

Twenty years later, Mr and Mrs Trellis, as I now call me and my husband (nobody can buy as much garden trellis as we do), have a dog. So now it's Mr, Mrs and Billy Trellis.

At the time of writing, he has been with us for only one day and one night. So far, he has behaved impeccably. Apart, that is, from tearing up copies of both *Private Eye* and *The Oldie*. Perhaps he hates satire, or lacks a sense of humour.

I am determined to let Billy know that Mrs Trellis is not a woman to mess with. Further chewing of satirical magazines will be severely punished, as will all infringements of the Trellis's disciplinary code.

The mode of punishment has yet to be decided. I understand that hitting a dog on the nose with a rolled-up newspaper has been outlawed by the European courts. King, a crossbred Alsatian, brought a civil action against his owners, claiming post-traumatic stress syndrome after being belted with the *Independent*. It was a landmark case and has thrown us dog owners into a state of confusion. Now, when Billy looks up at me with those limpid eyes of his, I wonder: is he looking at me with unconditional love, or because he is planning to speak to his solicitor after I accidentally trod on his paw? But there I go again, giving the dog human characteristics. He's only been here thirty-three hours. He doesn't know how to phone a solicitor. Not yet.

Madame Vodka

When I was at junior school, our teacher asked the class to work out how old we would be in the year 2000. The answer in my case was fifty-three years of age. At that tender, pig-tailed age, fifty-three seemed ludicrously old. Hardly human. When I allowed myself to think about a fifty-three-year-old me, I imagined myself as a type of space creature, similar in looks to the bulging-brained Mekon, but wearing a silver all-in-one suit with the obligatory pointy shoulders. I saw myself living in a glass tower in the sky, my transportation being a flying version of the Morris Minor.

As you can probably tell, I picked up most of my futuristic imagery from the Dan Dare comic strips, which I read surreptitiously, believing that they were written to be read only by boys. As a child I was full of such mad misconceptions. I constantly misread signs that read 'Trespassers will be prosecuted', reading instead, 'Trespassers will be *persecuted*'. For years I believed that if I accidentally strayed on to private property I would be captured, taken away and persecuted (i.e. tortured) by the indignant landowner.

Comics of the Fifties were full of stories about adult wickedness. I remember ballet mistresses and lighthouse keepers being particularly malevolent characters. However, my husband, who has just brought me a cup of tea and glanced at this page, insists, with some emotion, that the lighthouse keepers of his literary boyhood were entirely benevolent old blokes with white beards, Guernsey sweaters and wellingtons. I say that he is mixing up his wicked lighthouse keepers with his entirely trustworthy sea captain types. I defend my memory of wicked lighthouse keepers and he challenges me to produce a single example in children's fiction of a wicked lighthouse keeper. I rise from my desk and make my way to the room where the children's books are kept. However, I stop outside the closed door and remember that I have promised the youngest daughter that I will not go into this room. The reason is complicated, and involves two cats and a litter tray. I turn away from the room and go back to my desk.

My husband is in the living room, watching my favourite American sitcom. He is laughing and has obviously forgotten the lighthouse-keeper argument, whereas I am now obsessed with lighthouse keepers. Doubts set in. I consider calling friends. Am I confusing white-bearded lighthouse keepers with black-bearded smugglers?

I go into the living room to find my husband and Bill, the dog, asleep on the sofa. He jumps down guiltily as he hears my footfall: he is not allowed on the sofa. (The dog, not my husband. My husband is allowed on to the sofa in the evening, providing he has completed his household tasks.)

Perhaps I am on safer ground with ballet mistresses. They were certainly wicked, and figured pretty highly in the *Bunty* comic that I devoured each week. The ballet mistress always had a short Russian name prefaced with, of course, Madame. Let us call her, for the purpose of this article, Madame Vodka.

This severely elegant woman, her hair in a chignon, was only ever seen wearing a little black dress and carrying a stick. Nearly every week Madame Vodka would lose her temper and shout, banging her stick on the rehearsal room floor. 'Vi vont you dance, Engleese girl?' she would scream at a plucky ballerina with a secret broken ankle.

Occasionally Madame Vodka would be pictured in a private moment, quietly weeping over a photograph of a beautiful young girl in a tutu and a swan headdress. 'Olga! Olga! You ver ze best!' she would sob. Was Olga her lost, or perhaps dead, daughter? My schoolgirl heart would warm to Madame Vodka, until the last frame, when it would be revealed that – gasp! – the photograph was of Madame Vodka herself at the height of her triumph, before a broken ankle brought her career at the Bolshoi to a calamitous end.

The year 2000 is looming and I'm thankful that I escaped the pointy-shouldered silver baby-gro fashion as predicted in my youth. However, some change of style is demanded by the new century. I feel I should start planning my new image now, in the spring, ready for next year.

I'll need to grow and dye my hair for the chignon. I can easily buy a little black dress and the classic black court shoes. I'm quids in with regard to the angry expression and the walking stick. I wonder if I can persuade my husband to call me Madame Vodka? Just the once.

Spanish Restaurant

The husband and I went to a restaurant in Leicester called the Costa Brava the other Saturday night. Bullfighting posters decorated the walls, the décor was distinctly Spanish. Spanish artefacts littered the walls. A Spanish waiter took my coat. The Spanish maître d' showed us to our table, where ten of our relatives were already pondering the brusque English menu.

Main courses were Beef, Turkey, Lamb, Steak, Scampi, Chicken, Curried Vegetables. Starters were Soup, Grapefruit, Egg Mayonnaise. (This is a truncated version, but you get the picture.) When the waiter came to take my order, I asked if I could see the Spanish menu.

'No,' he said, 'we hain't got a Spanish menu. We hain't done Spanish for fifteen year.' (A spy tells me that they will do you a paella if you beg and plead and promise to keep the information to yourself.) I apologized for my faux pas in thinking that a restaurant called the Costa Brava, owned and run by Spanish people, should be expected to serve Spanish food.

'So, whatja gonna 'ave?' he said impatiently, lowering his

heavy brows. He'd got me down as a troublemaker, I could tell. 'The grapefruit and the scampi,' I stammered. Another waiter appeared and inexplicably removed all the wine glasses from the table. A howl of protest went up from the amassed relatives and the glasses were returned.

My husband asked for the wine list. Most of the listed wines had been scored out with a smeary black Biro. He made his choice from the handful remaining, only to be told by Señor Heavy Brows that these were also unavailable. My temples began to throb gently at this point. However, my husband remained cheerful and it wasn't long before we were drinking wine of such delicacy that one wag remarked, 'This must be the wine that Jesus made from water.' You could have given this wine to Winnie-the-Pooh or Po of the Tcletubbies without either of the creatures getting drunk.

The 'starters' arrived. My grapefruit was fresh, having recently left its tin. It was served in a tiny, stainless-steel bowl that could have served as a washbasin for Tom Thumb. It was garnished with half a tinned cherry. It was entirely delicious.

A musical duo took to the raised platform at the end of the room (to call it a stage would have been a gross exaggeration). They began to warm up. The dreaded strains of the electric synthesizer were heard throughout the land. A glitter ball began to revolve, and the two men crooned together to a synthetic bossa nova rhythm. It was harmless enough, but the cynics among us rolled our eyes around a bit and exchanged a few 'Oh-my-gawd' glances, then the main courses came out.

I have never, not even in the States, seen such vast quantities of meat. The steaks were draped languidly over the edges of the large plates. The beef, turkey and lamb were cut into thick slices, then stacked like a multi-storey car park. The chicken-eaters appeared to have whole, four-legged, four-winged birds to themselves.

Then the scampi arrived, crunchily delicious on the outside and moist and tasting of the sea on the inside. Incidentally, does anybody know where scampi is caught? Is anything known about its habitats or habits? Is it a tropical or a cold-water creature? Are there such things as scampi farms? Is it a fish or a crustacean? Does it swim in a shoal, or is it a loner? In 2,000 years, will it have evolved sufficiently to grow its own breadcrumb coating?

The leader of the duo, a man who looked amazingly like Dennis the Menace's father, urged us to sing along. 'We've got our mouths full,' shouted my relations and I, spitting food. Huge platters of glorious butter-coated vegetables were carried from the kitchen shoulder-high and served with commendable speed. Fat brown chips were distributed and made a noise as they were dropped on to the plate, thus passing the Townsend chip test.

Later we did sing, and we waltzed, and we frugged, and twisted, and did the Locomotion, and the Birdie Song and the conga, and, together with the other diners in the restaurant, we celebrated three birthdays and the passing of exams in midwifery and law.

As the night wore on, the duo excelled themselves, the glitter ball seemed to pick up speed, and I was ashamed of my earlier criticism. It was everything a Saturday night should be. I'm determined to have more of them. It sure beats reading Dostoevsky in bed.

Deadlines

By the time you read this, I will have finished a new book. I won't tell you the title, because I don't want to use this column to sell you anything, and anyway, the book does not go on sale until October 1999. So, I am working to a deadline. I have six weeks to go. There is no time to be ill, there is no time to stand and stare, there is no time to live any kind of normal life. Unfortunately, normal life does not know this, and it keeps tapping me on the shoulder, reminding me that it's there and asking me to come out and play.

This book dominates my every waking moment. My eyes open in the morning, and when my brain wakes, thirty seconds later, it immediately begins to mentally scan the written pages, finding mistakes and lost opportunities in the text.

I hold simultaneous conversations. Some are real conversations, with flesh-and-blood people; the others are inside my head, with the fictional characters who inhabit the book. It's no way for a grown woman to live.

The tension has to be released somehow. Some writers

resort to drink or drugs or serial promiscuity (or all three). However, the majority, according to my own straw poll, unwind by taking the dog for a walk, lying in the bath listening to Radio 4, having furious rows with their loved ones, smoking too much, or weeping uncontrollably because a stranger has been kind to them. There is only one activity of the five above that I do not indulge in.

There is, of course, another category of writers; writers who can live ordered and respectable lives. They go into their studies at 9 a.m., after bathing, eating breakfast and reading the paper. At 9.05 a.m., they are sitting at their word processors, writing. They break at 11 a.m. for coffee and a biscuit. At 11.15 a.m., they resume work. The only sound that can be heard issuing from behind their closed study doors is the clicking of keys as the book takes shape. At 1 p.m., they stop work, walk around a bit to stretch their legs, then go into the kitchen to have their lunch. They have excellent digestion. They also sleep well and enjoy busy social lives in the afternoons and evenings.

The people who belong to this category of writers are called men. I would like to be given honorary membership one day. The quality I most envy in men is their ability to concentrate on one thing at a time.

Women are notoriously able to 'multitask'. You only have to watch a mother of small children on a school-day morning to see these skills exhibited. With one hand she is brushing a child's hair, with the other she is tying a child's shoelace. Her left foot is kicking the dog away from the packed lunches, her right foot is pushing itself into her shoe (the right one, she hopes). One eye is watching the clock, the other is looking for the car keys. Her mind is dwelling on the thought that she should have gone to Goa with Dirk the hippie when he asked her to, rather than marrying Derek the surveyor and having two children. Her brain, however, is telling her that Dirk is probably in a drug rehabilitation unit somewhere, having lost both his sense of adventure and his exotic good looks, and that life with Derek, while not exciting, is at least organized. After all, in three years' time he'll be able to put a deposit down on that caravan he's been saving for since 1997.

God, how I envy my fictional Derek at this moment. I can see him in my mind's eye as he glides through his working day, doing whatever it is that surveyors do, moving calmly from one task to the next. Do thoughts of his wife and children cross his mind and impede his work? No. And, when he comes home, he leaves the surveying world behind him. He is at peace.

I cannot, in my present frame of mind, achieve this: I am maddened by deadline neurosis. So, let smug Derek enjoy his life a moment longer. I will visit a curse on him that will destroy his happiness for ever. I will plant the idea inside his head that he is capable of writing a book: a novel that explores the sex 'n' sleaze underbelly of the surveying profession. And, as if that weren't enough of a curse, I'll give the poor schmuck a three-month deadline.

As I said at the top of the page, by the time you read this I will have finished the book. But until then, it is going to give me an enormous amount of pleasure, and release a lot of tension, to think about poor, doomed Derek, struggling with his deadline.

Winnie-the-Pooh

I met a woman on a Greek island last year who had never heard of Winnie-the-Pooh. She was English. She was in her middle fifties. She was educated, a graduate.

I know that, like me, you are reeling in amazement, saying, 'How can this be?' But it's true. This lively, literate woman had never heard of one of Britain's literary icons. It is the equivalent of stumbling upon somebody who has never heard of Shakespeare, or Elvis, or the Eiffel Tower. These things are in your face, whether you like them or not. This woman's blind spot was revealed in front of a large group of people. I had referred to Pooh Sticks, the game Pooh and his mates invented. (You throw sticks into a stream on one side of a bridge, then run to the other side to see whose stick comes through first.)

The woman interrupted my talk. 'Excuse me,' she said, 'but what is Pooh Sticks?'

I explained.

'But who is Pooh?' she said.

'Winnie-the-Pooh,' I said.

'But what is he?' she said.

'He's a bear of very little brain,' I said, quoting from a Pooh book.

The group, all aspiring writers, tried to help the woman thinking that she had suffered a temporary memory loss. Various key names were contributed: Eeyore, Piglet, Kanga, Roo, Christopher Robin. The woman was still puzzled. The group tried harder, quoting favourite lines. A Scandinavian woman doctor was particularly good at this. The educated Englishwoman listened as though we were speaking in Martian. 'But you have children,' one of the group said, accusingly. There was an underlying feeling that this woman had deprived her children of one of the essentials of life. On a par with food, clothes, daylight.

I speculated to myself about the woman's life. Had she been brought up in a closed religious community like the Amish, where references to the outside world were carefully vetted? It appeared not. Anyway, Winnie was incapable of offending anybody's sensibilities, wasn't he? Winnie put the 'a' in anodyne. He was hardly a boyz 'n' the hood, street struttin' kinda bear, was he?

The more the poor woman protested her total ignorance of Winnie, the more I realized the full extent of the Winnie-ization of our culture. This idiotic bear's image decorates a child's bowl I have had for thirty years. This is the only piece of memorabilia I have in the house. However, go to the city-centre shops and you will find Pooh is everywhere: on duvet covers, pencil cases, lunch boxes. He is in book shops. He is a car sticker, a balloon. He is on television, he is a film. He is an hilarious and moving talking book, read by Alan Bennett on Radio 4. He makes a fine teddy bear: cuddlier than his well-travelled rival, Paddington. But far more importantly, he is part of our culture. He has been assimilated into the English language, as have his friends.

Example: 'No, we won't give the ambassador's job to Hetherington; he's a bit of an Eeyore.' True, Pooh's power base is with the upper, middle, and aspirational working classes. But this woman was middle class. She bought books and read them. She listened to Radio 4. She knew all about opera and sun-dried tomatoes.

She has no explanation for her lack of Pooh-consciousness. To comfort her I told her that, until recently, I had believed that birds – all birds – slept in their nests at night. This was less comforting than I had hoped. Most of the group were under this misapprehension, and some were horrified when I told them birds slept on the branches of trees. There were cries of 'Poor things,' and 'Why don't they fall off ?' A question I was unable to answer.

I knew that once the woman returned to England, she would be inundated with Pooh imagery and references. Would she turn into an infantilized devotee, or would she revile Pooh for his gormlessness? Because Pooh is stupid beyond belief and a lazy greedy-guts *par excellence*. He is, in many ways, a bad role model for today's school-inspector-driven, late-nineties children.

However, when I become a bear of very little brain, when I'm dribbling in the corner of an institution, I hope someone brings in a Pooh Bear for me to cuddle. He may be thick, but he's gentle and kind, and, in the end, that's all that matters.

My Place is Three Stars

I'm here in Cyprus finishing a comic novel. It's a grim business writing comedy, especially when you write as I do, in those small, dark hours of the morning, between midnight and five. I'm staying in an apartment-hotel on the beach. The crashing surf and the sound of the tiny pebbles being dragged back and forward by the sea is a constant backdrop. In the first few days before I got used to the loudness of the sea I occasionally grabbed at the TV remote to try to turn this sea noise down, like a modern-day Canute.

I started out the week in the hotel next door, a five star, but I flounced out after a young waiter stopped me leaving the breakfast room with a cup of coffee. 'I'm going to drink it outside,' I explained, nodding towards the terrace where the sun had come out and the flowers were blooming. 'No, you can't take the cup outside,' he said. 'If I break the cup I will pay for the damage,' I said, smiling, though my teeth were beginning to grit. It was not exactly *High Noon*, but it was a definite stand-off – me with my cup and saucer, him with his laden tray.

'Look,' I said, 'I'm fifty-three years of age. I know how to hold a cup and saucer.'

'It's against the rules,' he said.

They'd already got me down as a troublemaker. I had previously asked for a kettle in my room and been told 'no'. They'd then relented, but said I must give them a £20 deposit – 'as protection against theft'. I pointed out that I could buy a brand-new kettle for £17, so there was no reason why I would need to steal one of theirs.

I'd also objected to the nasty little laminated note next to the minibar, which said: 'Guests must not empty the minibar and substitute their own food or drink. For unconsumed items taken from the minibar there will be a charge of 45 cents per item, per day.'

Show me a person who drinks exclusively from a hotel minibar on a fortnight's holiday and I'll show you a lunatic. A can of Coca-Cola sold for 35 cents in the supermarket outside was transmogrified into a ludicrous £2.50 inside the minibar. I rang down to reception. 'Could I have my minibar cleared?' I asked. 'I'm a diabetic and I'll need to stock the minibar with sugar-free drinks.'

'There will be a charge,' the girl on reception said.

I told her that I'd read the notes, but that I was a diabetic. I was asking for my fridge to be emptied on medical grounds. She wouldn't budge, so I went through the ridiculous subterfuge of emptying the minibar, stashing the contents in my suitcase, substituting my own food and drinks (butter, cheese, a jar of Haywards Piccalilli, Ry-King, Diet Coke, Diet Sprite) and then reversing this procedure before the minibar checker called on the room with her clipboard and pen. It's no way for a grown woman to behave, is it?

Another thing I had against this hotel was that the pool

man was a sadist. By ten o'clock in the morning, most of the families were settled on their sunbeds around the pool: fathers reading their two-days-old *Daily Telegraphs* (hotel price, £3), mothers slapping Ambre Solaire on to their plump white inner thighs, the children in their swimsuits teetering on the edge of the pool, some clutching their blow-up pool toys – armchairs, dinosaurs, rings and so on.

'Why were they teetering on the edge?' I hear you say. 'Why weren't they in the pool, splashing, laughing, learning to swim?'

The answer is, because the pool man didn't start to clean the pool until ten o'clock. And then he cleaned it slowly, oh so slowly, and sometimes, having cleaned it once, he went around with his pole and net and cleaned it again. Any child who dared to put a tiny toe in the water incurred his wrath. 'Wait! You must wait,' he shouted.

Meanwhile, I kept myself from exploding in anger at this restrictive practice by writing a letter of complaint in my head to the hotel manager. 'Do you realize that your guests are not able to use the swimming pool until eleven o'clock in the morning? Blah, blah, blah.'

I didn't send the letter because I would have hated the pool man to get the sack. I checked out and moved to the three-star place I'm in now, with an empty fridge and a stove where I can cook my midnight feasts and a pool where there are a few dead insects on the bottom and a lot of flower petals floating on the surface, but which is full of happy children at 8.30 in the morning, and where the pool man has a foot pump to inflate the plastic toys.

I know my place, and it's got three stars.

The List

I've been asked recently to contribute to a book of advice for young people. I felt like writing to the organizers and advising them that young people don't read advice books – they think they know everything there is to know in the world. They also think that anybody giving advice is, by definition, not worth listening to. But who can resist giving people of any age the benefit of our experience and wisdom? Not me, so here goes. These are not in any order of importance, as will become obvious.

1 Only wear white socks if you are playing tennis.
2 Be aware that 'coffee' is a codeword for sexual intercourse.
3 If you call your daughter Victoria or Samantha, she will grow up to call herself Vic or Sam.
4 All young women should own a Swiss army knife – the one with the screwdriver, tweezers, nail file, can-opener and corkscrew. It should be kept in their handbag at all times.
5 All young men should own a Swiss army knife, but they should not take it out of the house or they will be arrested for possessing an offensive weapon.

6 Stop drinking alcohol the moment you are unable to pronounce the word 'succinct'.

7 If you enjoy doing everything in the most difficult way possible – whether it's working, studying, socializing or travelling – get pregnant by an unreliable youth and have his baby.

8 Read for at least an hour every day.

9 Remember that all governments tell lies.

10 Women should carry a pair of flat, black lightweight sandals in their bag at all times.

11 Save up (even if it takes you two years) and buy a simple, black V-neck cashmere sweater. It weighs practically nothing, it's not bulky, it's warm and it will withstand neglect and abuse.

12 Do not buy expensive jewellery. Somebody will only take it away from you.

13 When travelling, always buy a local newspaper (even if you can't read the language). You can sit or lie on it. You can use it as a plate. You can use it as toilet paper. You can shelter under it and keep your head dry. You can roll it up and swat insects with it. You can hide behind it. The uses are endless.

14 Bear in mind that the fire brigade has been busier since it became more fashionable to bathe by candlelight.

15 Use a shoulder bag or rucksack that is big enough to carry 5lb of potatoes home.

16 Eat a raw onion and raw garlic every day if you are tired of being pestered by men.

17 Before going abroad, have ten one-dollar bills sewn inside each of your bras. This will be enough to enable you to eat, drink and telephone the British Embassy to tell them about the theft or loss of your money, passport, credit cards and plane tickets.

278

18 If, at seventeen years of age, you have a little monkey tattooed on your belly, stop to consider that, by the time you are thirty-one and nine months pregnant, the little monkey will have stretched to look like King Kong: not a pleasant sight for the midwife.

19 Nose studs *always* leave a hole in the nose, ask my daughter, Victoria.

20 Wear thong-type knickers when wearing trousers.

21 Ask questions. And talk to strangers.

22 Always choose an aisle seat on aeroplanes.

23 Try to get part-time work as a waiter or waitress. You will learn several invaluable things: how to deal with drunks, the secrets of the professional kitchen, and how to behave in restaurants.

24 If your parents complain about the vileness and untidiness of your room, buy a padlock and keep the key on your person.

25 Never shave your eyebrows off. They will grow back in laughably eccentric shapes.

26 If your boyfriend thinks that Valentine's Day is a conspiracy led by florists and card companies, ditch him immediately. (He's probably right, but ditch the miserable git anyway.)

27 Remember that the average can of pop contains six spoonfuls of sugar.

28 Don't believe the shop assistant when she tells you that you look 'amazing' in the sludge-green tent dress you tried on for a laugh. She is just really desperate to reach that month's sales quota.

29 Never choose a fixed set of Lottery numbers.

30 Never read advice columns. They are inevitably written by middle-aged women with a grievance against the young.

Mrs Magoo

Hello *amigos.* **Due** to diabetic retinopathy I am now partially sighted. It is an interesting condition to have and means that I am forced into bumbling around the world looking slightly more of a fool than I was before.

Eccentricity is creeping up on me. I now have two items hanging from my neck: my tinted prescription spectacles and a large magnifying glass.

Without these two items I cannot read newsprint or normal-print books. This is a mixed blessing. Since I was eight years old I have been addicted to print. I would clean my teeth with a book propped against the basin. I read in the bath. I couldn't go to the lavatory without a book. I read on my way to school, in the cloakroom, at the table. I couldn't eat without reading.

I took a book with me to the delivery room and read throughout the labour until I started screaming too loudly to be able to concentrate on the words. I still remember a terrifying rail journey from London St Pancras to Leicester in 1987. I'd forgotten my book; I faced two hours without anything to read. It was the equivalent of a heroin addict undergoing cold turkey. I walked up and down the train searching for print. Eventually I found a four-page pamphlet stuffed between the seats: *The Campanologist*. I fell on the bell-ringing news and chitchat like a starving dog on a bone.

I used to read for at least four hours a day. The retino-pathy has relieved me of this time-consuming habit. I say 'relieved' because it has to be admitted that not all the reading I did was pleasurable. I was a print slut. I would read anything, anytime, anywhere: the *Beano*, the *Spectator* and the Kellogg's cereal packet; the instructions on the back of an Immac box and the small print in insurance policies. If there was graffiti in a lavatory cubicle I had to read every word, and sometimes even corrected the spelling and punctuation.

I can still read my own writing because I write with a thick black pen on white paper, though I cannot see the ruled lines on the page easily. But who cares? I am fifty-three years old and there is nobody to rap my knuckles for going over the edge of a line.

I call myself Mrs Magoo after the myopic Mr Magoo, the cartoon character who fumbled his way around town and country falling down manholes and mine shafts.

Farce is never far away. I recently threw a pair of yellow washing-up gloves on the compost heap thinking they were potato peelings. I tried to pay for a bottle of pop in Leicester with Cypriot coins. There is a danger that I will leave the house looking like Coco the Clown, due to an inability to see my face properly while applying make-up. Only the other day, on the way to the station, my husband said, 'Sue, I think you've put a bit too much rouge on your cheeks.' (He was born in 1950; he doesn't know that blusher is the new rouge.) I looked at my face in the mirror with spectacles 'n' magnifying-glass combo and was horrified to see our aforementioned friend, Coco, staring back at me, looking as though she were about to enter the big top.

There are many advantages to this condition. You can have a dog, but you can't see the dog hairs. The kitchen floor always looks clean; it's not until you feel the grit under your feet that you realize it needs a sweep and a wash. Your own body looks pleasantly airbrushed; the bumps, scars and horrible bits are mercifully edited out.

Because my grooming has become hit and miss I am now planning to pay professionals to do it for me. I will be coiffed, manicured, pedicured and eyebrow-tweaked by young women who can see what they are doing. I am leaving it up to family and friends to tell me when I have food stains on my clothing. I hope they won't be too polite about this. I recently walked around the city centre for an hour with black dye all over my face due to a leaking leather coat. A kind shop assistant in Boots finally informed me of this fact before handing me a wipe.

So *amigos*, a new and interesting life opens up for me. I now inhabit a world that is softened at the edges. I cannot see the details of faces, so loved ones will never age and fall into decrepitude. Everybody looks beautiful to me. Human beings are amazingly adaptable to changing circumstances: I've already forgotten the things that I thought I would miss.

So, if you see a woman walking towards you with food stains on her clothes, too much 'rouge' on her face and glasses and a magnifying glass around her neck, it'll be me. If you're a friend of mine and I cut you dead, don't take offence. I'm still Sue Townsend, but I'm also that other person now, Mrs Magoo.

Millennium

Do you remember this time last year? Millennium fever swept the land. We all had great plans to celebrate the end of a thousand years and to welcome in the next thousand. Then reality, that miserable spoilsport, set in: pedants wrote to the newspapers pointing out that according to the ancient calendars and the confluence of the moon, blah, blah, blah, the millennium was not due for two more years (or it had already happened, depending on which newspaper you read).

Some of our plans then were hopelessly ambitious. Ordinary British people talked of sipping cocktails on Bondi beach. Others talked wild-eyed (and after a few drinks) of hiring baronial halls in Scotland and filling the chilly bedrooms with 117 of their friends and relations – forgetting, in their millennial fever, that their mother was unlikely to bond with their friends, nearly all of whom had spent time in drug and alcohol rehabilitation units.

Some were aiming for the long-haul thrill option: bungee-jumping off Niagara Falls, swimming with sharks in the Red Sea, walking unarmed through the Somalian bush. Then they realized that the airlines were hiking up their fares by as much as three times, and so were forced to consider the 'staying in Britain' option.

Now I don't know about you, but I've been disenchanted and angered many times by the British hotel industry. In my view, *Fawlty Towers* didn't go far enough. I've spent too many hours in hushed hotel dining rooms with ancient waiters creeping along swirly carpets, carrying silver domes covering wizened chops and sodden vegetables. These hideous foodstuffs are served between fork and spoon, *à la* silver service, and are stone-cold by the time they hit your (cold) plate. I hardly dare step inside the dining room at breakfast time because of the toast factor. Call me capricious, call me demanding, but I like my toast to be served with my breakfast, not as a soggy afterthought.

The British are an extremely clever, innovative people. The list of our achievements is truly impressive. We produced Shakespeare, the jet engine and the Beatles, so why can't we ever get hot toast right? In your average hotel the toast is usually served just as you're about to rise to your feet and go to your room to start packing. As I walk down the hotel stairs towards the dining room I rehearse my speech . . . Me (to Ancient Waiter): 'Would it be possible to have my toast served at the same time as my eggs and bacon, please?' Ancient Waiter (looking alarmed): 'It's not our usual policy, madam.' Me: 'Yes. I realize that, but I'm asking you to break with years of tradition and serve the toast *with* the breakfast.' Ancient Waiter (shaking head): 'You'll have to talk to the manager, madam. It's more than my job's worth.'

Some people maintain that the millennium is nothing more than a marketing opportunity, hyped up so that we will be hypnotized into buying T-shirts, mugs and souvenir replica Domes. And, of course, this is true. We live in a world controlled by market forces. Were Jesus to be reborn today, you could guarantee that *Hello!* would have a fifteen-page spread of the event. Joseph would have his hair and beard styled by Bethlehem's most fashionable coiffeur, and Mary would be given a complete makeover and a personal trainer to get her figure up to scratch. Brooklyn Beckham has set a new standard for celebrity babywear, and Jesus's swaddling clothes would almost certainly be exchanged for something more cutting edge, in leather, or maybe velvet.

Hardly anyone I've spoken to intends going to the Dome (apart from a few Greenwich residents, who somehow feel a proprietorial fondness for the thing). This reluctance must be due, in part, to ignorance as to the contents of the big tent. I'm an interested person, but if I were to be tortured, I'd still be unable to tell you what exactly it is inside that's going to thrill and delight us once we've stumped up our twenty quid entrance fee. However, I am excited by the huge Catherine wheel that has been erected by the Thames. When lit, it will be a glorious and celebratory sight.

So, what are my own plans for the millennium night? The true answer is that I have none. I may make the ultimate sacrifice and baby-sit the grandchildren; we could have a midnight winter picnic, with fireworks, and joke about their parents. We'd then drive home to eggs and bacon and the first hot buttered toast of a new dawn.

Pink Elephant Car Park

Mr and Mrs Broadway had eight days in which to take a holiday. We sat at the kitchen table in Leicester and talked about where we'd like to go. Neither of us could look the dog in the face. He doesn't like us going away and punishes us each time we return by withholding his affection, Joan Crawford-like.

I remember that Mr Broadway once said, in the early days of our acquaintance, that he wanted to see Pompeii. Then I remember he has since sworn that he never wants to see an ancient monument or artefact for as long as he lives. He's not a Philistine. Have pity on the man: he was once exposed to about 2,000 icons in ten days – even the most zealous culture vultures on our Russian tour began to whimper with boredom as they were herded by a bossy guide towards yet another musty church full of priceless paintings. At one low point I thought Mr Broadway would commit slow suicide by taking off his hat, scarf, gloves and overcoat, and lying down in the 30°F-below-freezing snow.

So, I approach the subject of Pompeii stealthily, by filling his wine glass and mentioning that Italy would be warm at this time of year. He agrees. 'Where in Italy?' he asks. I lay a false trail. 'Florence?' I suggest. He says nothing, but I can tell what is going on inside his head, and it is this: he is tramping the hot-as-hell pavements of Florence with an inaccurate map, looking for a church, a gallery or a statue.

'No, not a big city,' he says.

'The Amalfi coast is beautiful,' I say.

'Amalfi,' he repeats. Again I see inside his head: he is imagining himself on a sun lounger, sipping Italian beer. He is surrounded by exotic-looking plants and Italian women. He is reading a blockbuster novel about the end of the world.

I refill his glass. 'Yes, Amalfi,' he says, dreamily.

Now is the moment. I strike. 'And Pompeii is nearby.'

'I've always wanted to see Pompeii,' he says, obviously forgetting his horror of historical monuments.

'We'll fly to Naples and stay in a hotel in Amalfi,' I say, confidently. We avoid the dog's gaze and go to bed.

There are no flights to Naples and no hotel beds in Amalfi. Which is why we find ourselves at the Pink Elephant Car Park at Stansted airport driving around section G in the rain. We are doing this because a computer ordered us to. Section G is obviously full. We pass a queue of angry passengers. They are wet and so is their luggage. They are waiting for a shuttle bus to take them to the airport, which is miles away. We disobey the computer and park in section H. Miraculously, an empty shuttle bus stops and picks us up. I cannot look as it drives past the angry queue in section G. But I imagine their howls of outrage. The Pink Elephant sign appears to mock us as we leave the car park. The creature is dancing on its hind legs, grinning and waving its trunk in the air. If I had been in the G-section queue I would have wanted to do serious damage to that Pink Elephant's happy face.

We flew into Rome, then hired a nippy car (an Opal) and drove along the perilous coast road to Ravello, where we stayed in a twelfth-century castle. On our first night, the townspeople greeted us with a spectacular firework display (that's my interpretation, my husband thinks our arrival coincided with the end of a religious festival).

After six days of heaven we drove back to Rome, calling in at Pompeii on the way. I couldn't help thinking, as I walked around the magnificent site, with its beautiful villas, grand amphitheatres, fountains and public swimming pools, that we have learnt almost nothing since about town planning. They had one-way cart roads, fast-food outlets and pubs that opened on to the street. And – who knows? – if Vesuvius hadn't covered the town in lava and ash, they may have invented the cappuccino. Mr Broadway was enchanted and we plan to go again.

We got off the plane to find that Stansted appeared to be in disarray. It seemed that hardly anything worked. Even the roller towels in the ladies' loo were on the floor. Pink Elephant Car Parks were in chaos again, due to the breakdown of their computerized credit-card payment system. To make things worse, I couldn't find an automated cash machine with any money in it.

When we eventually left the environs of the airport, I looked at the flat Essex landscape and thought that what was needed was a large volcano – an active one, with enough lava and ash to cover the smile on the face of that prancing pink elephant.

Solitary Behaviour

Writers spend much of their lives in silence. We spend our days in a room, alone, or in my case at a café table alone. Because, unfortunately, it is not possible to write and talk. So our vocal cords are hardly ever fully stretched. We may occasionally mutter a line of dialogue to ourselves, or let out the occasional curse of anguish or frustration, but we mostly sit in silence during the hours of daylight. I am an extreme case.

If I am at home I rarely answer the telephone. I jump when it rings, then stare at it with trepidation until it has stopped. Most callers give up after twenty-five rings. It is only my family, or those who know me well, who persevere. Sometimes, when the sun is shining and I'm feeling confident, I will answer it, but usually I will not.

This is infuriating to people who are important in my personal and working life, but I have resisted their entreaties to install an answering machine. I couldn't bear to hear their anxious voices asking me to phone them back 'urgently'.

If my husband is away I can go as long as three days without speaking to a soul – apart from the dog, who, although very intelligent, is an animal of very few, in fact, no words.

I do converse with *The Archers* on Radio 4. I shout at these fictional airborne characters seven days a week. 'As if,' I thunder at the radio, as yet another ludicrous story line is introduced to Ambridge's already gothicly melodramatic village life.

'Go back to drama school!' I order, as an English actor attempts a Canadian accent – and sounds like Dick Van Dyke in *Mary Poppins*.

But those dog and radio conversations leave barely a mark on the throat. Were Inspector Morse to examine my corpse he would be struck by the obvious under-use of my vocal cords. 'Lewis,' he'd say, 'take a look. This woman's hardly ever spoken. She must be a writer; it's our first clue.'

'But,' Lewis would stammer, 'just because she's under-used her vocal cords doesn't mean she has to be a writer, does it? She could be a nun who has taken a vow of silence.'

'A nun?' Morse would scoff. 'Look at her fingers, Lewis. What do you see?'

Lewis would blush and mumble, 'Nicotine stains. Sorry sir, yes, she must be a writer.'

And off Morse would go, driving his Jag around the Oxfordshire lanes, sometimes forgetting himself and reverting to being John Thaw.

Anyway, I think I've made my point – that I am not the chattiest of people. Ask my children. I used to communicate with sighs, or grunts, eye rolling or derisory snorts. It was tough for them, but it's given them something to kick back against – they all appreciate a good conversation now.

I now have no voice at all. My voice fled three days ago. It started grumbling when I did a book signing and spoke to over 150 people. (Please don't think this is typical. I've often sat in a bookshop and spoken to no one, apart from the embarrassed manager, and customers who asked me to direct them to the stationery department.)

The next day I was interviewed several times, becoming croakier and croakier until I was making sounds more like a crow than a human. At one surreal moment I was in a radio station being introduced to Meat Loaf, the booming-voiced singer of 'Bat out of Hell'.

His security man said, 'Mr Loaf, I'd like you to meet Susan Townsend.'

'Hello, Mr Loaf,' I whispered, with only a vestige of voice.

'Hello, Susan!' he boomed.

Apparently only his wife is allowed to call him Meat.

After he'd swept along the corridor with his entourage, it was my turn to enter the studio.

I was given a hot lemon drink and I sipped at it – while the traffic reports were read – confident that I would be able to make a reasonable sound. When the red light on my microphone came on, the presenter asked me a question. I opened my mouth to answer, but nothing came out.

She coped very well and improvised brilliantly, then took a deep breath and asked another question. My voice screeched and rumbled and refused to be controlled. We stared in horror at each other. Radio 5 Live listeners were probably blaming my vocal abnormalities on poor reception.

We staggered on; she was brilliantly inventive and articulate. I was too, but nobody heard me. The squeaks leaving my throat were unearthly and, with apologies to Mr Loaf, I sounded like an old bat out of hell.

Fed up

I'm fed up today. Not depressed, that's too dramatic a word to describe my mood. And anyway, depression is an illness and needs a doctor and medication. I don't need these things.

The weather is not helping; it's one of those gloomy days, still and grey. The air is damp, though it isn't raining – yet.

The news is of wars, earthquakes and floods. The TV screen shows images of men fighting and of women and children struggling to survive in impossible conditions. My speak-your-weight scales have just shouted at me that I am eleven stone, ten pounds, another cause for melancholy. Then there's Bill, the dog; he's gone lame again, the day after his check-up at the vet's, where he was pronounced to be in excellent health. He goes back to the vet's for an examination under sedation. And I've just read a review of my latest book that called it 'vacuous' and suggested I stop writing.

Another cause for my discontent is that I've just returned from London, where I trawled the shops for new clothes. I slid the hangers along the racks in increasing desperation. All the clothes in London are manufactured for exhibitionist seventeen-year-old stick insects. At my age (fifty-three), I need camouflage, not combat trousers. I need clothes that make my legs look longer, my stomach flatter and my figure like Sophia Loren's. What's more, I need these miracle garments to come in black, grey or white, and to be impervious to shrinkage.

Another worry is the growing pile of correspondence: each letter needs a personal reply, and one day, one marvellous day, I will write those replies and I will remember to post them. However, since that backlog encompasses seventeen years, that marvellous day will probably never come.

Work, of course, is always a cause of concern. At the moment of writing I have two imminent deadlines: the twentieth rewrite of a film, and a six-part television series. Each word of these scripts will be scrutinized and criticized. Is it any wonder that putting pen to paper brings me out in a nervous sweat?

Another cause for concern is my inability to cope with machines. I cannot fit a new ink cartridge in my fax machine. I do not know how to operate a computer, adjust the filter in the fish tank or set the timer on the video. I take no pride in these non-achievements. I do not consider myself to be above such practicalities, it's just that I can't grasp how to work the damn things.

You see, I am not a Millennium Woman.

On days like today I torture myself by cataloguing the various things I've lost over the years. It is an awesome tally: enough gloves to keep a family of octopus warm; enough umbrellas to keep the population of Borneo dry;

enough pens and lighters and scarves and sunglasses and cosmetics to stock a hotel shop.

Unusually, there are no family dramas taking place at the moment. Or are there? One never knows with grown-up children. They keep bad news from you. 'I didn't want to worry you, Mum,' they say when you discover their house burned down a fortnight ago and they forgot to renew the insurance.

The Next Day

The weather still has a long face, but my spirits have risen.

The dog is back from the vet's after examination. An x-ray has shown absolutely no reason for his limp. The vet thinks he is 'putting it on'. Why does the dog need to go in for this attention-seeking behaviour? He is constantly showered with love, affection and bones. I know he would prefer to be a human being, but he'll just have to come to terms with his role in life. Perhaps he should see an animal therapist, who can help him get in touch with his inner dog.

The Day After

Forget I ever wrote that protracted whine. I am a reasonably healthy woman, living in a peaceful country with electricity, clean water and food, and a husband who does his fair share of the housework. I have been in touch with each of my children; they tell me their houses haven't burnt down and I believe them. I am showered with blessings and full of optimism. And I hereby resolve to tackle the new technology. However, I'll take it steady. There's no point in running before I can walk, is there? Before I can surf the Net, I think I'll need to tackle the fish-tank filter.

Our Hospitals

Something that has haunted me for some time now is the callous treatment that some of our old people are subjected to in hospital. This is still something of a taboo subject because the orthodoxy is that medical staff, especially nurses, are angels, and as such are beyond criticism. Most nurses are hard-working, professional and kind, but a few are not, and these individuals can make life difficult for their colleagues and utterly miserable for the vulnerable people in their care.

It is generally accepted by people of my generation that the standard of nursing care in our NHS hospitals is lower than it used to be. I don't like the term The Good Old Days. Daily life is immeasurably better for most people today. However, there were Good Old Days for hospital patients. I know, because I experienced them. I was in hospital for various illnesses in my youth. And for those of you who are young today, let me describe how things used to be run on a typical NHS ward.

The ward itself was usually a long room lined with beds. It had large windows, giving natural daylight and an outside view. Those patients too ill to read or amuse themselves could lie in bed and watch the weather or the light change. They could also watch the never-ending traffic of the ward: the cleaners at work, the consultants' rounds, the drinks and drugs and meal trolleys, the comings and goings of the nurses . . . It was possible to see and hear everything.

Once patients were mobile they were encouraged to help dispense the beverages and help out in the ward kitchen, which freed the nurses for the job they'd trained for – nursing.

There was a rigid hierarchy of nursing staff on the ward. At the top was Sister. These formidable women wore a distinctive uniform and a frilly white cap, which was particular to the hospital and needed to be laundered and refolded daily. These Sisters were most definitely in charge. Their wards ran to a strict timetable, and followed a rigid routine of nursing care. Every morning each patient was given a bed bath and had talcum powder applied to pressure points. Our teeth were cleaned, our hair was brushed and we were helped into a clean nightdress. After our bed linen was changed we lay back on our snowy pillows like pampered kings and queens.

The Sisters were constantly on the prowl for bedsores, post-operative infections, and dirt. All were regarded as shameful occurrences. Elderly patients were propped up and fed at meal times, and would not be allowed home until they were eating well. It was a safe, open environment. Any unkindness from a nurse to a patient would have been noticed immediately and just as quickly stopped.

The last time I was in hospital was a deeply depressing and distressing experience. The ward was lit mostly by artificial light and was split into bays, which gave a feeling of isolation. There was a shortage of bed linen and not enough pillows. Nobody appeared to be in charge and there was often confusion about the correct prescription of drugs. Sometimes there was a multiplication of treatment. Several times it happened that patients would be nil-by-mouth all night, prepared for theatre, then told their operation had been cancelled.

Most distressing, though, was how some of the elderly on the ward were treated. I watched one very frail old lady who had been brought in to hospital from a local-authority retirement home, having broken her hip after a fall. I'll call her Mrs Young. She lay on her back, unable to see anything but the gloomy ceiling. She occasionally called out her long-dead husband's name. Meals were placed next to her on the bedside locker, where they stayed until the food grew cold and was taken away. Drinks were similarly placed out of her reach. She had to ask repeatedly for a bedpan. Many times it arrived too late and she had to lie in her own mess. Her face went unwashed and her hair went unbrushed. Nobody came to visit her. She, and others like her, were talked to disrespectfully and unkindly by her 'assigned nurse'.

I intervened on Mrs Young's behalf a few times but, trapped in my own bed, was unable to help her practically. There were many Mrs Youngs on that ward, and I'm still ashamed that I didn't complain officially.

After I left hospital I went back to the ward to pick up a discharge letter to give my GP. It couldn't be found. Neither could the prescription for the drugs I'd been prescribed. Mrs Young was still there, staring at the ceiling with her wild hair sticking up. I'd like to report that I went back and cared for her, but sadly I didn't.

Giving up

I don't want you to think that I spend most of my time in hospital, but I've been in again. Remember the Sydney flu? I went down with it on 11 January at two o'clock in the afternoon. Yes, I can be that precise because at five minutes to two I was as fit as a newly strung fiddle, but 300 seconds later I felt so ill I could hardly lift my head. The next day the doctor was called. He looked a bit peaky himself.

'I've been in bed with the flu,' he said, 'for five days.' He looked down at me sympathetically and added, 'I've never felt so poorly.'

'Five days!' I thought, as I lay back on my pillows. 'I can't spare five days. I've got places to go, people to see, scripts to rewrite.' I'm perpetually rewriting scripts. I compare myself to Sisyphus, who was condemned to a lifetime of pushing a boulder up a mountain, only to see it roll down again once he'd reached the top. As it turned out, the five days stretched into three weeks. I was one of the many who developed complications (pneumonia) and after a hideous time at home, was taken to a lovely white hospital bed, and the blessed relief of a saline drip and an oxygen mask. I obviously have an addictive personality, because I became overly fond of the oxygen, and the tubes had to be practically torn from my nostrils the day before I was discharged.

Three weeks is the longest I've been without a cigarette since I was fourteen. As I lay in my wonderfully comfortable hospital bed I tried to imagine what my life would be like as a non-smoker. The horror! In my mind I rehearsed entering a restaurant and asking to be seated in – I can hardly write the words – non-smoking.

All my adult life I have felt a mild pity for non-smokers, and wondered how they could deny themselves one of life's great pleasures. The smoking section of the restaurant seemed to have a jollier, and more animated clientele. There was more laughter, more drinking, more of everything. How would I feel to be parted from my kind of people? The motto of one half of my split personality (the Sue side) is 'too much is not enough' – would I now have to inhabit the puritanical, disapproving (Susan) side, motto: 'too much is sinful and wicked'?

I read in my newspaper this morning that cigarettes are as addictive as heroin and cocaine. It suggests that GPs should treat addictive smokers in the same way they treat alcoholics or drug addicts. Nicotine-replacement therapy should be available on the National Health Service, according to Professor Martin Jarvis, one of the Tobacco Advisory Group, who produced a report on behalf of the Royal College of Physicians.

I can assure Professor Jarvis that I am undergoing severe withdrawal symptoms. I may need to be strapped into a straitjacket, like Jack Lemmon in the *Days of Wine and Roses*, before I am addiction-free.

Trials and tribulations lie ahead of me. I'm doing OK in

the house where I write and spend most of my time, which in itself is a triumph: I used to light a cigarette to help me write a note to the milkman, and how will I be able to wander round the garden without a cigarette in my hand? And what about those long car journeys, when cigarettes were such a comfort? How will I cope with pavement cafés in Paris? How will it be possible to drink the delicious coffee without having a celebratory cigarette?

Professor Jarvis's report calls for cigarettes to be regulated like other drugs. This would only lead to a huge deviant subculture where tobacco fiends would hunt down their supplies. Tobacconists would become the new Mr Bigs of the criminal world. Underground clubs would open. They would be named things like Gaspers or Fags or even Chokers for hard-core addicts.

What would happen to a smoker caught possessing a packet of Silk Cut? Probation for a first offence; prison for a third? What would be regulated (banned) next? Sugar? Fat? Sunbathing? Climbing stepladders? Falling out of bed? Fireworks in the back garden? Crossing the road? Driving a car? Alcohol? All governments should be wary of banning anything. We, the public, need our small freedoms, our little pockets of rebelliousness. We do not enjoy being treated like children under the control of a Nanny state. Over-disciplined children tend to behave badly, once Nanny's back is turned. Forgive me if I sound a little irritable, it's just that I'm dying for a fag.

Size and Exercise

I've got a speak-your-weight machine. You step on it and an authoritarian, upper-class male voice shouts, 'Please step off,' then barks out your weight. Just lately it has been barking out horrific statistics, such as, 'Your weight is eleven stone four pounds.'

I haven't given the weight shouter a name. I don't approve of naming inanimate objects. I do not find it charming when people give me a lift in a car called Lydia, or refer to their washing machine as Mavis. I find it twee and irritating. In my experience 'Lydia' and 'Mavis' are always breaking down. I can imagine the foul language when the service engineers hear on the telephone that Lydia is slow to start, or that Mavis has stopped spinning.

I don't entirely trust the speak-your-weight machine. I think it is lying to me. How can I be eleven stone four pounds in the morning and eleven stone eight pounds before I go to bed? And anyway, how can I be eleven stone, never mind the pounds? I've been ten stone something for years.

All my clothes have been bought for a ten-stone-something woman. A size 12 was guaranteed to fit. Yet only the other day I was trying on a size 12 shirtwaister and couldn't get my arm in the sleeve. It was obviously a manufacturing fault, I thought. Some machinist somewhere in Taiwan, daydreaming as she stitched up the armhole.

I got dressed again, left the cubicle and snatched another size 12 shirtwaister from the rack. The same thing happened. I dressed again, went out to the shop floor and rifled through the rack for a size 14. Inside the cubicle I struggled to get it on. It strained across my back, the buttonholes gaped and it clung to my thighs like clingfilm to a microwaved chicken.

I dressed and left the cubicle again. A security guard watched me as I searched for a size 16. Security guards follow me around all the time. I'm used to it now. There's something about me and my behaviour that arouses their suspicions. My partial sight doesn't help. It makes me look slightly gormless and I blunder about a bit, as though slightly drunk.

There was no size 16 shirtwaister. I was secretly relieved, and I vowed on the journey home to stop eating so many fish-paste sandwiches. Yes, I know that other dieting women vow to give up chocolate éclairs, lager and other delights, but I've become addicted to fish paste: crab, salmon and shrimp, sardine and tomato. I guzzle them all. My husband buys them for me in trays of twelve at the garage that now serves as our corner shop. He buys so many jars that the girl behind the counter now gives him a discount.

'Is your wife pregnant?' she asked one day. 'No,' he replied, 'she's stopped smoking.' The girl understood – she's a smoker herself and saw the connection between nicotine and fish paste. A non-smoker would probably have thought the two substances had only a tenuous link. So, consumption of fish-paste sandwiches had caused me to balloon in weight. The only clothes I can get into are the baggy black trousers and loose tunic tops meant to disguise thick waists and fat bums, but which in fact shout: 'Look at me, everybody, see how fat I am underneath these baggy clothes!'

I will join a gym, I say to my husband. I will get up at six every morning and, after a healthy breakfast of nuts, grain and fruit, I will walk to the gym, exercise for an hour and walk back. He looks at me with pity in his eyes, and doesn't even bother to respond. Though later, when I modify my proposed exercise regime and ask if he'll give me a lift to the gym, he smiles and says that he will.

It is true that, to date, I have yet to visit the gym, or even telephone to request membership details, but I will one day. When I am thinner and fitter, and have more energy and my breath doesn't stink of fish paste.

Since I stopped smoking cigarettes, I have been lighting other things such as candles and fires. This is pathetic compensatory behaviour, I know, but I like the merry crackle of the fire in the grate and candlelight is enormously flattering to a person who has just been told by a bossy speak-your-weight machine that she is eleven stone and four pounds.

Water Features

I was slightly ashamed when I saw that my husband had written under a Saturday in my diary, 'Day off with my husband'. I've been working long hours and weekends for months. The film (*Adios*) is now in its twenty-third draft. A French film director once said to me apropos of *Adios*, 'Suzanne you are either ze genius or ze idiot.' This was a few years ago when I was a delegate to a screenwriters' workshop held in a château in Bordeaux.

At the time I preferred the genius option, but now I know for sure that I am 'ze idiot'. The problem with a screenplay is that if you start to mess about with it, the whole thing unravels like a homemade cardigan and you have to re-knit the damn thing together again, only to find that the wool is kinky and twisted. This film is now such a part of me that I may have the title tattooed on my forehead.

On the morning of my Saturday off I woke to a sunny day. After breakfast and the papers, the plan was to drive around the countryside, and find a shop that boasted in the Yellow Pages, 'We are the biggest stockists of water features in the East Midlands.'

Don't laugh, we live in landlocked Leicester, miles from the sea, and we're fond of a bit of water. Actually a decision had been made to turn the greenish thing we laughingly call a lawn into one vast pond.

It's Bill the dog's fault. He sometimes forgets who he is (a Labrador retriever) and takes on the persona of world champion greyhound. He runs around the garden thinking he's at White City, and has consequently scored a deep circular track in the lawn.

The English countryside seemed to be populated by large numbers of black people. I was pleased to see this evidence of integration and said so to my husband. He looked around, puzzled. 'I can't see a single black person,' he said, as we passed through a village. A peculiar thing had happened to me – a combination of sunshine and diabetic retinopathy appeared to give everybody a dark skin colour. My dream of racial integration was an optical illusion.

We arrived at the water feature centre to find security fences and closed-circuit television cameras. Notices bristled in the car park warning us not to steal the plastic pond liners. The door to the shop was rigged up to an incredibly irritating bell that rang six times whenever anyone entered or left the showroom.

There were many water features around. Various attempts had been made to recreate nature in the raw. Plastic herons poked their beaks into reconstituted stone streams. A plaster badger stood on a hummock of Astroturf next to a fibreglass brook. The badger appeared to be watching the false lily pads jerk about in the fierce current caused by an over-eager water pump. It was profoundly depressing. I thought fondly of the brook near to where I lived as a child and of how delicious the water tasted when we lay on our bellies to drink it on a hot summer's day.

By now it was lunchtime. We ate fish and chips in the chip shop car park. We threw most of ours away. The batter was soggy, the chips were languid, and the vinegar was not the real thing – it was that brown stuff they make from recycled sump oil, and call 'non-brewed condiment'.

We drove on to an organic farm shop, which I will call Growing Anxiety. My dream of returning home with the fruits of the earth withered, like the vegetables, which were on the rotten side of wizened. A man in a jolly shopkeeper's outfit panicked about change when handed a five-pound note for two wholemeal loaves (one of which went spectacularly mouldy after two days).

We left the farm shop desperate for something to eat. My husband satisfied his hunger with an ostrich-burger in the grounds of a country house, where a Country Food Fair was being held. As we ate we watched a puppet show. A man in Marks & Spencer leisurewear had sewn two black felt circles for eyes on to a yellow sock. He put the sock on his left hand and called it Jeffrey. He spoke to the sock and the sock spoke back, sounding exactly like the man. In the end it was impossible to tell where the man ended and the sock began. A small crowd watched in embarrassed silence.

A highlight of the day had been visiting a wood yard and buying six bags of logs. But, despite newspaper, kindling and firelighters, the logs refused to burn. It would seem that in the countryside even the trees have lost heart and had enough.

Boot Sale

I've just finished a piece of script so difficult that I thought my brain would explode with the effort. A younger, fresher writer could have knocked it off within normal working hours but, in my present enfeebled state I have had to work all day and sometimes all night.

Weekends have not existed; bank holidays have come and gone. My grandchildren have grown tall in my absence. My grown-up children seem to have aged alarmingly. I haven't even visited the gym that I vowed to join months ago. In fact, I've hardly left the house in months. Months.

I allowed myself only one visit to the cinema to see *American Beauty*, but even this brief foray into the world had to take place late at night, when the rest of England was thinking about bed. I'm not asking for pity; I have chosen to work in a notoriously difficult area – screen-writing.

Someone recently described films as being made by crazed perfectionists and, at times, I have fitted this description perfectly. I have been known to sit and stare down at a piece of paper for hours, stuck on a single line of dialogue.

Anyway, *amigos*, at four in the morning the latest draft of a film was completed and I went to bed after sipping a glass of champagne with my husband and my working partner (two different men).

The next morning, Saturday, the script was re-edited and then e-mailed to various interested parties. And I sat out in the garden blinking in the sun, like an animal newly woken from its hibernation. I slowly recovered. I did things that normal people did: brushed my hair, watched Jerry Springer, watered the plants, fed the fish and slept. Then, on Sunday morning, the smell of bacon brought me downstairs and my husband announced that he was taking me to a boot fair.

I gathered up the odd coins I keep in little pots around the house, and off we went to pillage – to buy containers for plants and large plates for drip trays. We were not fussy about the form these containers took, almost anything big enough to grow runner beans in would do. However, old galvanized buckets were my ideal.

Two huge fields were chock-a-block with the detritus of people's lives. A few were operating from the boot of the car, but most had set up wallpapering tables. A few superior types were sitting in their motorized homes, while their children did the dirty business of selling.

Regular readers will perhaps recall that I am Mrs Magoo now, due to diabetic retinopathy. I do not see fine details. I recently served a friend a piece of cake covered in ants. He very graciously said that he needed more protein anyway, but you get the picture.

I couldn't see most of the stuff on sale unless I peered at it from a distance of inches. This disconcerted some of the sellers; perhaps I looked like a CID detective trying to identify stolen property. Incidentally, there was a dispro-portionate number of youths selling lawn mowers and garden tools; they wore baseball caps and dark glasses, and smoked cigarettes in the style affected by those used to slopping out in prison. They were not the type of healthy-complexioned lad one naturally associates with the open air. I couldn't help but be a teensy weensy bit suspicious that the prevalence of garden theft and the rows of lawn mowers at the boot fair were in some way connected.

There were catering vans selling cheap, fast food. There was a toilet block with a permanent queue, but it was mostly gloriously disorganized. There were no officials to boss us about and, of course, we, the public behaved impeccably as we usually do when left to sort ourselves out. I hope the day never comes when a miserable spoilsport government brings in legislation to control boot fairs. Most of us follow the rules for six days a week, so please continue to give us a small break on Sundays.

Here is a list of our swag: a doll's pram, without mattress, but with naked occupant – a matted-haired doll; a portable radio with new batteries; toy dressing table – with working lights surrounding mirror – stool and hair dryer; heavy-duty toy Tonka tipping truck; six dinner plates; a reclining garden chair and fifteen plants; lithograph of African river scene; ten A4 exercise books; twenty Magic Marker pens and 100 envelopes; five old galvanized buckets; one pig's trotter (smoked); a plastic watering can.

Now, this is my kind of capitalism.

Burial

We were walking around an exhibition at the Islington
Design Centre. There were three floors full of covetable
things, ranging from furniture to candle holders. For an
ex-shopaholic like me, it was a testing time. My interior
designer daughter, Lizzie, was looking for flooring. Her
company is called Cactus Designs, which goes against the
current fashion for feng shui. Feng shui practitioners abhor
cacti and ban them from their non-prickly interiors. I'm
proud of the girl for swimming against the tide.

'My God,' I said to her as we approached one stand, 'that
green coffee table looks like a coffin.' This observation may
have come out of the side of my mouth, but it was loud
enough to have been overheard. The casually stylish salesman came up to me.

'It is, in fact, a casket,' he said. 'It's called an Earthsleeper.'
My daughter and I laughed rather nervously as he extolled
the benefits of this biodegradable product. I can do no
better than to quote from the brochure. 'The Earthsleeper
newspapier-mâché coffin has been created for those seeking
a simple, elegant, affordable and environmentally friendly

form of encapsulation for burial. This easy-to-assemble flat-pack casket comes complete with natural muslin body covers.'

This was no laid-back hippie-run organization. Their corporate clients include the Co-operative Funeral Service and Office World.

The endorsement of the Co-op did it for me. They have always despatched our family efficiently and respectfully, and if the Co-op thought a paper coffin in red, blue, green or charcoal was a suitable container for a loved one's body, then it was all right for me. I asked my daughter if we should order one, but she persuaded me against it, saying there were choices of size and colour that were best made at home.

There comes a time in every parent's life when a change-over occurs. One moment you're telling your child to wear a vest, the very next, it seems, they are advising caution over your choice of coffin.

Another product on the stand was a Petpeace – a smaller version of the Earthsleeper for pets. I'm thinking of getting one for Bill, our dog. This is ludicrously morbid. The dog is in vigorous health, does not dash across main roads and is only two years old, but even so, it's as well to be prepared and I'd sooner that Bill was interred in our garden in a Petpeace, than wrapped up in an old blanket and bunged into a hole.

The last funeral I went to was that of my ex-sister-in-law, Wendy. She was a remarkable woman who was born with Down's syndrome. She lived a life of admirable independence, travelled widely, did a parachute jump and had a part-time job as a shelf stacker (the Co-op, again).

Wendy's funeral was conducted by a clergywoman,

Jayne, in a beautiful old church, St Andrews. The service was lovely. There was none of that censorious 'born in sin, died in sin' orthodoxy, which is the last thing one wants to hear when one is grieving for a loved one.

After some traditional hymns in the church, we went to the crematorium. Our two nine-year-old granddaughters had been prepared by Jayne for what would happen there. They conducted themselves with great dignity, as their great-aunt's coffin disappeared behind the curtains to the sound of Elvis singing 'You Were Always on My Mind'.

After the ceremony there was much talk among the mourners about the type of service we would like for ourselves. Most people seemed to want a mixture of traditional and popular music. Somebody said to me, somewhat naively, 'The right words are so important on these occasions, aren't they?' And of course they are. In a church or similarly atmospheric place, each word rings out and is listened to with full attention. The wrong word can lead to disappointment and sometimes disaster.

A few years ago I went to a funeral where the vicar called the dead person by the wrong name throughout. Nobody in the church had the temerity to correct the fool. Nervous giggles swept around the pews and even the widow shook her head and smiled; though she had plenty to say at the funeral tea afterwards.

The words on a gravestone are particularly important. I've already chosen mine: 'Here lies Susan Townsend – half woman, half desk.'

Talking Books

A year ago I received a Talking Books tape machine in the post from The Royal National Institute for the Blind. The day it came I got into a huff and sent it back. 'I'm not blind, I'm partially sighted,' I stormed to my husband. 'Why don't they give the damned machine to somebody who needs it?'

In my mind's eye, I was thinking that this needy, abstract person would be totally blind; someone who lived in a dark world, where the only colour to be seen was black. I was taking the absolutist, Stalinist, line on blindness – the one shared by the majority of the population. It was a knee-jerk reaction, based on ignorance and probably fear.

My sight had deteriorated slowly, almost imperceptibly. Newspapers went unread, new books were bought, but never opened. Colours faded and my chair crept closer to the telly. My husband began to read aloud the subtitles of foreign films.

The partially sighted world became normal to me. As I've written before, there were occasional embarrassments: not recognizing friends, bumping my head on the glass of shop windows, stumbling off a kerb. But these were minor inconveniences, easily laughed off with the remark, 'I'm half blind.'

Then, over the course of one weekend recently, I went three-quarters blind. The tiny blood vessels in my left eye bled and completely obscured the retina. Imagine a thick black and red cobweb covering a camera lens – that's what it looked like to me.

At Casualty I was told that the blood clot would probably break down over a period of two to four weeks. There was no treatment, and my best course of action was to buy a pair of very dark glasses. I walked out of the hospital into bright sunshine, holding my husband's arm. I could not have walked to the car park without him. At an optician's on the way home I chose a pair of Dolce & Gabbana sunglasses, though 'chose' is not exactly the right word because I couldn't see them.

'How big is the logo on them?' I asked my husband nervously, as I stared sightlessly into the mirror on the shop wall.

'You can hardly see it,' he assured me, neglecting to tell me that Dolce & Gabbana is emblazoned in gold letters on both sides of the dark brown frames. A fully sighted person would be able to see this subtle logo from one end of a three-acre field.

So, in very dark glasses, with limited vision in my right eye and none in my left, I was unable to focus, read or write. By a cruel irony, I was due to visit the RNIB headquarters in London on the Monday after my 'bleed' (as it's referred to in the eye trade), to record an introduction to a recording of *Adrian Mole: The Cappuccino Years*, being produced by the Talking Books service. A fax was sent on Sunday cancelling the ten o'clock appointment.

At 10.20 on Monday the RNIB rang. 'Shouldn't you be here?' asked a polite young man. He hadn't seen the fax. I explained my new circumstances. Immediately sympathetic, he broached the subject of the Talking Books tape machine I had rejected angrily a year before. Did I want it back?

It arrived two days later, a chunky grey lump of metal with large buttons and a single lever for on/off and play. It couldn't be simpler to operate. Talking Books tapes arrived almost daily. I'm currently reading (or rather, listening to) my favourite books, John Updike's *Rabbit* quartet. These make up twenty-one and a half hours of unexpurgated story, and are read by an American actor in a relaxed manner. The process has been a joy and a revelation, and I'm spared all that tedious page-turning.

For almost a month I blundered about. During this time, I made only one long journey alone (from Leicester to Paddington) and found it exhausting, though I was thrilled to have achieved it. Before I left the house that day, I considered whether or not to bring my white stick with me, worried that strangers would see it and assume I was completely blind. Fate intervened. The granddaughters had been playing 'blind girls' with the stick, and it was lost.

My eye is nearly clear now, and I can see to write this in my usual thick black capitals. But my episode has taught me that if I ever did lose my sight completely, I would, with the kindness of friends and strangers, be able to enjoy life, if not to the full, then at least to three-quarters of the way up the damned glass.

November is a
Cruel Month

November is a deeply unpopular month. February doesn't excite much enthusiasm either, but at least its arrival means that spring is around the corner, that buds will soon be budding and that lambs are due to frolic briefly in the fields, before the mint sauce is put on the table.

November, however, has very little going for it. Mellow October with its rich colours and woodsy smells has sidled away and left bleak winter. The days are short and the sun can hardly be bothered to get up in the morning and go to work. The weather is cold, but in these days of global warming not cold enough for the spectacular frosts of my childhood that transformed the dull walk to school into a magical journey through a glistening white landscape in which every shrub, gate and lamppost took on a new appearance. It was like seeing plain Jane Eyre in a white sequinned evening frock.

I'm usually on the side of the underdog so I would like to stick up for November. I look better in winter clothes. Layers of wool are far more flattering to the middle-aged body than the flimsy wisps that summer demands. I like big wrap-around coats and clumpy boots and scarves and woolly tights. I would also like to wear knitted hats, but since a group of young men jeered at such a hat (at 5.30 p.m. on Christmas Eve 1996) I haven't dared. I've lain awake for many nights wondering about the above incident, asking myself why they chose to mock my hat. I now think that, in the frenzy of Christmas shopping, I may have been inadvertently wearing the hat back to front or inside out, or both.

I like returning home in November. The kitchen is always warm because of the Aga. This range is no longer a thing of beauty: it is scratched and battered, and the grease on it could co-star in a film with John Travolta. My Aga would never feature in an article in *Aga Magazine* for Aga owners – not unless it was steam cleaned by men in breathing hoods and overalls. But it still throws the heat out and is more welcoming than a radiator.

In November I can light fires; fire lighting is one of my few hobbies. In another life, given a few twists of fate, I might easily have been an arsonist. Every child in the 1950s knew how to light a fire. I have happy memories of kneeling in front of our fireplace in the breeze-block-built prefab reading the *News of the World*, before crumpling it up and laying sticks of kindling on top of its shocking stories of adult misbehaviour. Sin and flames, a heady combination.

I like November food – dark, rich stews, dumplings, mashed potatoes and cabbage. Then there's Bonfire Night when families reject our government's advice and turn into pyromaniacs. Watching television is better in November. This is nothing to do with the programmes (though we are spared the tinselled dross of Christmas specials, which are filmed in July anyway). For some reason it's more pleasurable to watch television when the nights are long and the outside world seems remote and alien. November is also conducive to lying on a sofa and reading a book, or simply staring into space. It's a winding-down month during which the word lazy should be banned from the lexicon.

When I am the Great Dictator of Britain, I will create a two-day holiday in the fourth week of November. These days will always fall on a Monday and Tuesday. On Holiday Monday everyone in the land will have to stay in bed and catch up on their sleep, or their lovemaking. (Small children will be given a mild sedative to keep them prone.) On Holiday Tuesday women will have to remain in bed, though men will be obliged to get up and do a little light housework and cooking. Coincidentally, it is on Holiday Tuesday that heterosexual men will be reminded what a toilet brush is. A government leaflet will have been posted to each household. The graphics will show which end of the toilet brush to hold, and which to plunge into the toilet bowl.

When I come to power, November will be a Christmas-free zone. No images of Christmas – Santa, reindeers, baubles and so on – will be allowed in the land. Even robins will be required to wear camouflage on their red breasts until midnight on 30 November. Somebody has to stop Christmas from leaking into surrounding months. It's profoundly depressing to be in a store shopping for a Guy Fawkes mask, only to stumble across Santa in his grotto.

So, instead of longing for summer (which so often lets us down), let us try to enjoy November. It may be dark, cold and forbidding, the Mr Rochester of the calendar. But at least it's not December. Now that truly is a turkey of a month.

Dennis's Presents

At this time of year, I recall the story told to me by Dennis, a waiter friend of mine, who used to work in a Soho club and restaurant. From 1 December until Christmas Eve the restaurant and bars heaved with private parties. The staff were run ragged trying to cater for their demanding and drunken guests.

They worked double shifts, sometimes not finishing until 3 a.m. Dennis described how he would fall exhausted into his bed only to wake seemingly five minutes later to begin another shift. One year, his mother wrote to tell him there was to be a family reunion in Sligo – forty-seven members of the family were to be there. Dennis's family were big on Christmas: they gave each other lovely, carefully chosen presents.

We all have our role in the family, and Dennis's was that of the black sheep. His mother disapproved of his job and considered he had wasted his academic talents. His nine brothers and sisters had respectable professional careers, earned substantial salaries and basked in parental approval. They had also provided them with many beloved grandchildren, whereas Dennis was gay and unlikely to provide them with a single one.

Dennis resolved to spend his wages and tips on buying forty-seven fabulous Christmas presents. He was naturally a spendthrift, but he saved his money and made a list, intending to buy a few presents every day. These gifts would have to be easily transportable because his journey entailed catching a tube train, a train to Holyhead, a ferry, a train to Dublin and a train to Sligo.

However, as the days of December passed and Christmas Eve, the day of departure, loomed, Dennis had yet to buy a single present. It was not until 23 December at midnight that Dennis realized with horror he would have only two hours the next morning before he had to catch his train. Instead of going home to rest, pack and prepare for the shopping marathon, he stayed up late drinking and bemoaning his fate. He slept late, woke in a panic and left the house on Christmas Eve morning without a bag or toothbrush.

'I'll buy a change of clothes on the way,' he thought, but presents were his priority. Foolishly he went to the West End. Idiotically he went to Hamleys toy shop on Regent Street. He had forgotten his list and fought his way through the heaving crowds of frantic parents and over-excited children, grabbing at anything he could reach. He chose very unwisely: heavy things, large things, difficult-to-carry things. Now for the adult presents. He staggered up Regent Street looking wildly in shop windows (those he could get near to). His bags were a burden. He barged into any shop he could get both himself and his bags into. Once again he bought anything he could reach or afford.

Meanwhile, the clock was ticking horribly fast towards his departure time and his bags proliferated and grew heavier. He became drenched in a panicky sweat. He knew that if he missed a certain train he would be spending Christmas at Holyhead ferry terminal alone, apart from his bags.

Eventually he realized he had reached the absolute limit of what he could carry. The nearest tube station was beyond his reach. After many tortuous minutes of failing to stop a black cab, he started to weep. Unable to put his bags down, his tears went unwiped. His sweat dried. There had been no time to buy new clothes.

A miracle happened: a black cab stopped and the driver got out and helped him with the dozens of bags he'd accumulated. He only just caught the train to Holyhead. His account of dragging his bags across the station concourse towards the soon-departing train was painful to hear. His entire journey home was the stuff of nightmares. Grimm's fairytales come to mind.

A young man tries to redeem himself and is given a task: to struggle with intolerable burdens (the bags) across hostile terrain (London to Sligo) against a strict deadline (Christmas Day).

When he eventually arrived at his parents' house he was greeted in amazement by the forty-seven. They were not only shocked by his dishevelled, wild-eyed appearance, but the fact he had bought them all a present. 'Did I forget to tell you?' said his mother. 'We agreed to buy no presents this year; we've all given £25 to War on Want instead.' Dennis was so exhausted by his ordeal he slept for most of the holiday.

Vodka

There's an extremely good bar in London called Tsars. It's situated in the Langham Hotel in Portland Place and is notable for the loud laughter heard spilling from it as one approaches. Mr Broadway and I had occasion to stop at the Langham Hotel recently. I was undergoing some medical treatment to my peepers at a nearby clinic and Mr Broadway chivalrously escorted me.

As part of his duties, he steered me into Tsars. There is, you may have guessed, a Russian theme to the place. Over seventy vodkas are available. Mr Broadway is an aficionado of vodka, not in a staggering around the streets way, you understand, but in a quiet, appreciative way. I've encouraged him in this occasional activity. I think everyone should have a hobby, especially husbands and partners. It takes their minds off the fact that you're no longer in the kitchen for most of the day.

The first night we went into Tsars we were comparative vodka innocents and, faced with a list of seventy, we needed help from our red-sashed waiter. Unfortunately, charming and eager to help as he was, our waiter was unable to advise. He was Brazilian and it was his first day. So we jumped into the vodka menu with both feet and without guidance. We floundered a little, not knowing quite how to manage the conical glass or the small ice-filled vase in which it came. There was obviously an etiquette to be observed. I failed to observe it and ended up spilling ice and cold water down my chin.

I used to be a frequent visitor to the Soviet Union. I went so often that one of my sons was convinced that I was a spy. After all, hadn't the name of one of my most popular fictional characters been Mole? Our first impressions of a country are usually accurate, and my first impression of the Soviet Union was that this was a place that teetered on the edge of chaos and was only held together with vodka. When Gorbachev made changes to the law governing the sale and manufacture of vodka, his government fell and Yeltsin, a notorious drunk, took over.

There used to be spectacular drunkenness in Moscow. In one of the hotels I stayed in it was customary to have to step over the doorman to gain entry after midnight. It was common to see his recumbent uniformed body sprawled on the floor blocking the doorway. The first time I came across this human barrier, I assumed he'd collapsed and looked for the arrival of medical assistance. However, realization dawned after a few moments of watching other guests manoeuvre around the body.

Vodka represents goodwill and fraternity in Russia and at most meetings there are long speeches and many toasts during which Russians congratulate themselves on their soul. It can get tedious. After listening to a series of officials banging on about Russian souls all day in a small provincial town, Alan Bennett muttered aloud, 'Oh, arseholes!' Mr

Bennett's tongue had been loosened and lubricated with many small glasses of vodka, otherwise he would, I'm sure, have remained as enigmatic and sweet-looking as ever. Incidentally, Alan Bennett is one of the few people I know who could literally *die* of boredom. Provincial dignitaries uttering platitudinous gobbledegook about Soviet/British friendship had him chewing his blue handkerchief in an agony of ennui.

I would contend that in a country as difficult to live in as Russia, it is essential that supplies of cheap vodka are available. For most of the population life is a daily struggle, and although one would like to believe that art and culture alone can ameliorate misery, one knows (in one's soul) that strong liquor can also do the trick in half the time and without having to book tickets.

Russian winters are so cold that diesel freezes and bus drivers have to light newspaper torches under the tank to thaw the fuel. One of my most vivid memories of Russia is standing by a bus in a temperature of 32 degrees below, while the driver lay in the snow and performed the unfreezing-diesel trick. When he had managed to get the engine running and the passengers had all climbed back on board, he sat behind the wheel and, with frozen fingers, managed to unscrew the cap of a silver flask before tipping his head back and glugging down the vodka inside. In Britain the Health and Safety people and the police almost certainly would have been alerted, but in Russia the poor bloke had simply done what he had to do to survive.

Winkle-pickers

I think it's time I employed a personal shopper. On a recent trip to London, I spent half an anxious hour in Richmond buying a collection of items that broke every clothes-shopping rule. They were the wrong size, the wrong pattern, the wrong style and, of the six items purchased, only two could be worn together. I even broke my own rules: will I wear the ruffled blouse with the flower pattern, or the brown and black hoop-striped woollen two-piece?

Even as I paid for the items, I knew my new size-16 bum would stretch the skirt to breaking point, and would make me look like a barrel on legs. But the thin French woman in the shop was so full of admiration when I stepped out of the changing room in the barrel she even put her hand up to her mouth. At the time I took this gesture to be an indication of her delight at the vision in front of her. But on reflection, a few days later, I now think she was probably trying to hide a smirk.

The brown woollen suit with the long jacket was bought to hide the size-16 bum, and it looked rather dashing beneath the bright lights of the shop. As I strode around the changing cubicle, striking poses to the strains of Charles Aznavour singing 'She', I could see myself walking along the Left Bank of the Seine in my new suit, which I planned to accessorize in a clever Parisian way.

I now realize the brown suit is beyond help. Attempts to cheer it up are rejected. It is suffering from clinical depression. Only a course of antidepressants and ten sessions of Gestalt therapy can help the thing. The multi-coloured woollen scarf with the beading and sequins appealed to me at once – as it might to a toddler. Indeed, a toddler had possibly made it at nursery school. This scarf can be worn with none of my new clothes. And I suspect my old black clothes won't want to be seen dead with it.

I can't bear to think about the cowboy boots the French woman was so ecstatic about when I tried them on. 'So flattering to the foot,' she said excitedly. I should describe these boots. In one respect they are your bog-standard cowboy boots: black leather, a comfortable stack heel and calf length. What made them attractive to me were the long snakeskin-patterned winkle-picker toes. I was fortunate enough to be a teenager during the winkle-picker era, when social cachet depended on the length and pointedness of the leather at the end of your feet. These shoes are what keep present-day chiropodists in business.

So why did I, a supposedly mature fifty-four-year-old woman, stop even for a moment to admire these boots? It was the French woman who made me try them on. 'I 'ave a pair at home,' she (no doubt) lied. So far, I have only worn these boots in my room at Pope's Grotto Hotel in Twickenham. They almost broke my neck. The winkle-pickers are inflexible and force one to plod along in a flat-footed way, as if crossing snowy terrain in snowshoes.

The boots are going back for a refund, as is the flower-patterned, ruffled blouse. I am, however, stuck with the dull brown suit and the striped woollens because these have been worn once (and already look years old).

Will a personal shopper save me from myself? Or will she look at my tired face, make assumptions and go out on to the shop floor to select a collection of pleasant clothes suitable for the young pensioner? Perhaps I should give in gracefully and accept that plain black, white and grey are the only colours I should wear.

As for sequinned scarves, the damn sequins go everywhere. Which reminds me of a story told by a woman of my acquaintance. She grew suspicious that her husband was having an affair when she saw him in the shower with a single sequin stuck to his bum. He could not satisfactorily explain its presence there. Since she owned no sequinned clothing, relations between them grew strained and eventually reached breaking point.

PS: You may have wondered about the derivation of the name Pope's Grotto Hotel. So did I. I asked a local taxi driver. 'It's named after the Pope, who hid there when it were against the law to be a Catholic,' he informed me. Wrong, as it turned out. Pope's Grotto Hotel is named after Alexander Pope, the poet, who lived nearby. How we deceive ourselves.

Third Draft

Believe it or not, this is my third attempt to write this article. The first two drafts (one written in a field, the other in a Wimpy) jumped out of my bag and ran away. Perhaps they've joined up somewhere and are enjoying each other's company; slagging off my spelling, punctuation and grammar.

I am writing this article in my hotel room at 6.15 a.m. I don't intend to leave the room until it's finished. The door is locked and the window is firmly closed. The article has no escape route. When it is finished, I shall trap it inside an A4 writing pad and take it to be faxed. Perhaps I should take no risks and employ Securicor to escort it to my editor's office at Sea Containers House, by the Thames.

Even as I write, I can feel the article struggling to be free. It wants me to write about something else. It wants me to show my character in a good light. It doesn't want me to harp on about my foolishness, or carelessness. It wants me to write exquisite prose about Love and Death. Failing that, it wants an amusing story about my dog, or a why-oh-why piece about domestic appliance repair men who failed to show up.

345

The first article I wrote was about filming *The Cappuccino Years* for television. As far as I can remember, it tried to be entertaining about the difficulties of filming in November (floods, leaves, mud, lashing rain) while pretending it is actually May 1997 (warm sunshine, cherry blossom, New Labour, new optimism). This first article banged on about me working with a team of sixty people and contrasted this with my usual working experience, which is sitting in a room, alone, for most of the day, and often part of the night. It was a very dull article. The cliché count was extremely high. I'm not in the least bit surprised it ran away before I could finish it.

The second article was about that good old stand-by, restaurant and hotel food. It was, in fact, a why-oh-why piece. I seem to remember that the article went on drearily about bad food, cold food, terrible food, greasy food, dry food and soggy food.

I was writing it in a Wimpy because they at least know how to cook a fried egg and toast. They can also keep the tables clean and the staff still have time to be kind to toddlers and the elderly, and to a mad-looking woman scribbling in a notebook with a pen clearly marked 'plant marker pen'.

I got to know the Wimpy in Teddington when my husband and I were passing in the rain on one of those precious days off. My husband stopped, looked in the window and remarked approvingly that the Wimpy looked exactly as they had done thirty years ago. Before we could stop ourselves, we were pushing the door open and sitting down. Unlike most fast-food places, there was no unpleasant smell wafting about. The menu is friendly to people. It allows variation, everything is cooked freshly, so your Wimpy bun will not be soggy with condensation. The puddings include traditional favourites such as banana split and spotted dick and custard, the cutlery is metal, and your tea comes in a proper cup or mug.

They don't throw much food away at the Wimpy in Teddington. I was surprised at how many completely clean plates were going back to the kitchen. Somebody has obviously worked out what a normal person with an average appetite can eat, unlike some restaurant chains that boast about their 'huge portions'. It is incredibly depressing to see people wading gloomily through overflowing platters and then see them falter halfway through before coming to a queasy stop, still with a mound of food in front of them. Anyway, article number two rambled on much in this vein. Again. I'm not at all surprised it did a runner.

Here, at this point, with 671 words written, I'm tempted to stop writing and go for breakfast. If I scrambled into my clothes I could just about make it to the hotel dining room before their 9.30 deadline, but I will have to resist the temptation; I have to stay on this article's case. Imagine if, while I was at breakfast, one of the non-English-speaking chambermaids ignored the 'Do not disturb' sign on my door and came into my room. After trying my clothes on, and using my cosmetics (yes, I know you do this chambermaids. I have watched many spy movies and know about the single hair trap), what if she saw this article lying on the dressing table and, not being literate in the English language, mistook it for rubbish and threw it away? What a disaster that would be. What a loss for English literature! No, I'd better stick it out to the end.

Wayne Webb

It was raining heavily in Soho, and I was tired. It was too much effort to put one foot in front of another. When I saw a row of empty chairs under the awning of a pavement café, I sat down and lit a cigarette.

Soho offers rich pickings to street beggars; the place is bursting with affluent workers who have well-paid jobs and liberal consciences. It wasn't long before a voice interrupted my stupor.

'Can you spare a cigarette?' I looked up to see an untidy, youngish man with long unwashed hair. There was something wrong with his face: it looked as though somebody, a practical joker, perhaps, had drawn circles on it with a red felt-tipped pen. When he moved into the light I saw that his face was disfigured by crimson sores.

I gave him two cigarettes and apologized because they were menthol. 'S'alright,' he said graciously, 'I can take the filters off . . . You look tired.' I needed to tell somebody about the bad day I'd had. Somebody who didn't know me, and wouldn't worry too much. He sat down next to me and, while he skilfully removed the filters from the cigarettes, I gave him a breakdown of my day. In the course of my account he suddenly said: 'You're Sue Townsend.' He looked pleased with himself. I agreed that I was Sue Townsend, but told him that today that fact gave me no pleasure at all.

He told me that he'd read my books when he was younger. 'Me an' Adrian are the same age,' he said. He began to talk about Adrian Mole, Adrian's family, Adrian's chaotic life. 'I'm saving up for *The Cappuccino Years*,' he said, 'but as soon as I get the money together, it goes.' He gave a helpless gesture, as if the money had legs and had leapt from his pocket and round the nearest corner. I could guess where the money went – not on booze. There were none of the usual signs of chronic alcohol abuse, but he was almost certainly no stranger to other substances.

His name is Wayne Webb and he is twenty-eight and a half – I was very touched by that half. He has been on the streets for ten years. His mother died when he was small and he didn't get on with his stepmother. He talked about his father with great affection. He sees him three times a year. 'My dad worries about me,' he said sadly. 'He wants me to pull myself together, you know what I mean?'

I could imagine what it was like to be Wayne Webb's dad, lying awake wondering how his boy was, if he was still alive. 'I wun't be here now if I'd gone to art college,' he said. 'The school told me to go, but I didn't know how to get in.' For years he'd collected his own drawings of London buildings in a folder. Architecture is his passion. 'I know every building in the West End,' he said proudly.

One night he'd booked into a hostel. In the morning the rucksack containing his folder had been stolen; he hadn't drawn anything since. Life has been hard since the sores appeared on his face. People keep their distance, his takings are down. He is worried that the shopkeeper who allows him to sleep in his doorway every night will get fed up and move him on. 'Good sleeping places are hard to find, you can't just sleep anywhere,' he explained. 'Everywhere is somebody's territory, and there's some rough people on the streets.' I could tell that Wayne Webb would be hopeless in a fight. I refrained from giving him advice; who am I to give anybody advice on how to live their lives?

At one point a tall, well-dressed American man passed us, shouting mad obscenities and barking like a dog. Wayne watched him compassionately and said: 'Poor bloke, that barking gets him into a lot of trouble.' Two days later, as I sat in Pizza Express, I saw the barking American being wrestled into a police car. He barked madly throughout the struggle.

It was unsaid, of course, but both Wayne and I knew that I would give him some money before he left. He talked about getting a job, a flat and a girlfriend, but somehow I could tell that he'd already given up trying to attain these goals. We talked about books for a while. He did a lot of staring into bookshop windows, and he sometimes turned up at book signings to have a look at the author.

A girl came out of the café and began to take the chairs and tables inside. As I fumbled in my bag for money to give Wayne, he looked away, politely. I gave him twenty pounds. He bent down and kissed me; I consider it money well spent.

Train Journeys

I don't keep a diary. I couldn't possibly risk my private thoughts and feelings being read one day. But I'm very tempted to keep a log of my train journeys from Leicester to St Pancras and back.

Entering a carriage is like entering a theatre to watch a play that you know nothing about. The mobile phone has added an extra dimension to the drama. I get into carriage 'A' at the very end of the train, where the despised smokers are now corralled. A small girl is wailing in pain and holding her ear. Her mother is trying to comfort her. They look frightened; both are thin and pale and skimpily dressed, considering it's below freezing outside and the countryside is covered in sparkling frost.

The ticket collector comes along and the girl's mother asks him if he has any painkillers. She tells him that her daughter has an earache. He is sympathetic, but explains that he is not allowed to give drugs to passengers. After he has gone, the mother takes out her mobile phone and calls somebody named Rose. Over the sound of the little girl's crying, she tells Rose that she's on a train to London, and asks Rose to go round to her house and remove her clothes and furniture, 'while 'e's at work'. She tells Rose that she has not paid the rent on her council house for four months and that, when Dave finds out, he will kill her. She then starts to cry.

From the ensuing conversation I find out that Dave is Rose's brother, and that both women are afraid of him. I can't bear the misery of it and prepare to get up and sit with the pair, but another woman slides into the seat opposite them and offers the girl a pack of Polos and gives the mother a tissue.

When we arrive at St Pancras I'm alarmed to see that the little girl has no gloves or scarf, and is bare-legged. The mother struggles along the platform with a heavy suitcase and a pile of carrier bags. I try to take a few of the bags, but the mother refuses. I fear for both of them as they walk out of the station into London. They are on my mind all day as I try to write jokes.

I catch the 8.25 back to Leicester that night, and am happily settled with a take-away cappuccino. Diagonally opposite me, across the aisle, is a middle-aged man with a bad haircut and unfortunate glasses. He is reading the *Evening Standard*. As the train leaves the station, his mobile rings. He listens to the person on the end of the line for a few seconds, then says: 'Oh my God!'

I look across, but my lousy sight prevents me from seeing the expression on his face. He then says: 'It said: "Hello sweetheart, it's me. I love you, and I miss you." ' Apparently this was the text message that he'd left earlier in the day on his lover's mobile phone. Her husband had found it and was demanding to know who 'me' was.

The train goes through three tunnels as it leaves London

and communication between the lovers was cut off. I waited impatiently for them to reconnect. She, it transpired, was in a public phone box with a pile of pound coins, and her husband was in the marital home with the children, her mobile phone and the incriminating message.

A story was concocted. Bad Haircut urged his lover to stay calm. 'Tell him it must be a wrong number,' he said. 'And keep to the story . . . Don't, for Christ's sake, tell him about me.'

As the train passed Luton, the lover left the phone box to get more pound coins. At Bedford his phone rang yet again. He asked his lover: 'Can you trace who sends a text message?' They discussed this; neither of them knew how the technology worked. Their paranoia increased.

The man had completely forgotten that he was in a railway carriage with at least thirty other people, all of whom must have been as transfixed as I was by his conversation. He was immersed in the psychodrama of his life.

At one point he broke from speaking to his lover and phoned his wife. The line was engaged. Was his wife being informed of her husband's deception? At Kettering, Bad Haircut said to his mobile: 'You know I love you, don't be a prat.'

Infuriatingly, it was impossible to tell whether he was speaking to his lover or his wife.